EARTH CHANGES BIBLE

A PERSONAL GUIDE TO THE COMING GLOBAL TRANSFORMATION

DIANE TESSMAN

INNER LIGHT PUBLICATIONS

THE EARTH CHANGES BIBLE

A Personal Guide to the Coming Global Transformation

ISBN: 0-938294-53-9

Manufactured in the Unites States of America

Editorial Direction:
Timothy Green Beckley

Cover Art: Barbara Lynn

Inside art courtesy:
Carol Ann Rodriguez, Merrilie Miller, Patricia A. Davey

Composition, layout and design:
Della Van Hise
P.O. Box 688
Yucca Valley, CA 92286-0688

For permission to reprint specific portions or to inquire about foreign rights, address request to

Inner Light
P.O. Box 753
New Brunswick, NJ 08903

Free catalog of books upon request

Contents

DIANE TESSMAN

PRELUDE

Something is up! Regardless of your walk of life, everyone agrees that as the Twentieth Century draws to a close, the Earth is going through dramatic, revolutionary, and frightening *changes.*

If you are a scientist or someone who is committed to following logic and intellect, you sadly accept the fact that the polar ice caps are melting. Global warming's imprints are everywhere, at every time of year; the summers are too hot and the winters are like The Ice Age. There is either too much water causing floods and coastal inundation, or too little water resulting in droughts and wild fires.

The planet's rain forests have been depleted to such a degree that the lungs of the planet are severely damaged. And you accept that the ozone layer has gaping holes allowing dangerous radioactivity to shower down upon us, with cancer and immune deficiency diseases increasing dramatically.

But perhaps you are a person who follows intuition first.

Perhaps you are a person who listens to "spirit." In this case, your psychic alarm bells have been ringing urgently for years now as you foresee all we have just discussed, and more.

With your psychic pathways open, you know the potential for very severe earthquakes has greatly increased. You watch as volcanic "rings of fire" awaken across the globe, and you *knew* they would!

You not only realize what is happening to us as a planet, you have seen it coming! You have read the ancient prophesies which tell of catastrophic events in the last years of the Twentieth Century but you have hoped beyond hope that a bright new reality can be created which has no basis in the current reality. Otherwise, you realize that Doomsday may well be at hand.

On top of Mother Earth's anger, we know that political institutions have become very unstable. Huge, established countries like the Soviet Union and Yugoslavia have simply fallen apart. We know that Social Security and Medicare are going bankrupt, and these are but two examples of a similar "unravelling" in the United States. Will the U.S. remain as one country?

The political situation has certainly gotten incredibly bad and unpredictable, whereas a few short years ago, we felt established institutions would always be there.

Financial fortresses have gone under. Well established companies are bankrupt while strange, shadowy multinational corporations take over.

Do a handful of super-wealthy men really run the world with allegiance to no one and nothing other than retaining their own power?

For most people, the urgent important question is, will my currency continue to have some value or is it possible the entire money system will just collapse? And how am I to honestly make money ever again as one door after another closes to my efforts at employment and enterprise?

There are very few jobs anymore. Bank tellers and supermarket clerks are being replaced by robots. The un-alive world of cyberspace is the only place there is any life. In the 1960s, when there was a real life for the working individual, a man who collected garbage for the city could make a decent living for his family. Then the large cooperations bought the garbage business, and now the pick-up workers get very little pay while the big boss at the top walks away with a fortune. This syndrome has been repeated over and over again in a huge variety of businesses within our culture. We now have a society which places no value on the human being.

What else was society created for? It was indeed created to serve the individual, to make his or her life better. Something needs to change drastically!

As if these threats, both natural and human-made, were not enough, we all fear what The Virus may do to the human race and to other life forms on the planet. AIDS. Ebola. Flesh-eating diseases. Super-tuberculosis, created by a wedding of virus and bacteria which is antibiotic resistant. And we are told that this is just the tip of the iceberg. Will we all succumb to mutating killer viruses soon?

Nothing short of a *brand new dimension* will solve the problems which face us now. There is not one but a number of crisis which threaten *all life* on the planet.

The slate needs to be wiped clean. The world needs to start over!

Is this what God is doing?

Can you as an individual survive this slate-cleaning?

This book will draw an outline for you about what is really happening in these cataclysmic days; we will make sense of what is happening.

And then, with shared understanding, we will offer you as an individual, a blueprint for surviving these severe Earth Changes.

Helping us will be higher beings from Space/Dimensional Intelligence, with whom I have had telepathic contact for years.

I channel Tibus, my star guardian, on a regular basis; I first encountered Tibus during two childhood UFO encounters which I remembered under hypnotic regression with Dr. R. Leo Sprinkle. This is detailed in my first book, **The Transformation.**

We will also have channeled messages from higher beings whom have sent special messages for the readers of this book. They are anxious for you to have the vital information which they transmit!

Join us as we seek to beat the odds and survive Doomsday!

Diane Tessman
P.O. Box 1802
Joshua Tree, California
92252-0857

February 14, 1996

THE BASIC 12 EARTH CHANGE PREDICTIONS

There will be so much chaos and momentum during upcoming Earth Changes that literally thousands of predictions could be made. However, we have been told by our friends in the higher realms that there are **12 Basic Earth Changes** which we must outline for you.

The Change Times will occur because of a mushroom effect, one event leads to the next one; or, several events will happen at the same time, creating such chaos that the planet will leap onward to the next major predicted catastrophe.

1. Global warming will snowball, with both the North Pole and the South Pole melting. Only 25% of the ice now at the polar caps will remain; the rest of the water from the ice will flood the oceans, seas, rivers, lakes, and streams of Earth. After mass flooding, islands will disappear, coastlines will be washed away, and sections of entire continents will sink under the rising waters. The face of the planet will be forever changed!

2. The greenhouse effect will also intensify to a horrific degree. It and global warming are, in fact, nearly the same phenomenon, but in order to perceive the enormity of what is happening, we will consider them separately, although acknowledging that they are thoroughly interlocked. The decimation of rain forests around the globe adds to this dreadful situation.

Remember that the greenhouse effect began when Earth was still perfect. Then the atmosphere started becoming impure and full of poisons, humidity intensified and caused rain clouds, leading to floods. However, now, the greenhouse effect is being heaped upon itself, because the planet's atmosphere and weather are no longer perfect! Poison air is added to poison air. Dense humidity is added to dense humidity. Rain comes down, adding to already rising waters. And there are few rain forests to give us fresh oxygen, and intake the carbon dioxide. This is what we mean by global warming and the greenhouse effect *snowballing.*

3. This *snowball effect* is in itself a huge threat because upheaval and destruction will become accelerated. Time itself will become accelerated; this has already begun. What began as a slight change in the weather will become, almost overnight, the reason for global chaos and catastrophe.

4. As huge chunks of land are swallowed up by rising waters which had been frozen in the polar caps, new nations will spring up, only to fall again. There will be sweeping political instability and upheaval. As part of one country floods permanently or sinks, neighboring countries will fight for "ownership" of what is left; they will try to take-over what remains of the government. Earthquakes and volcanic activity will affect these remaining

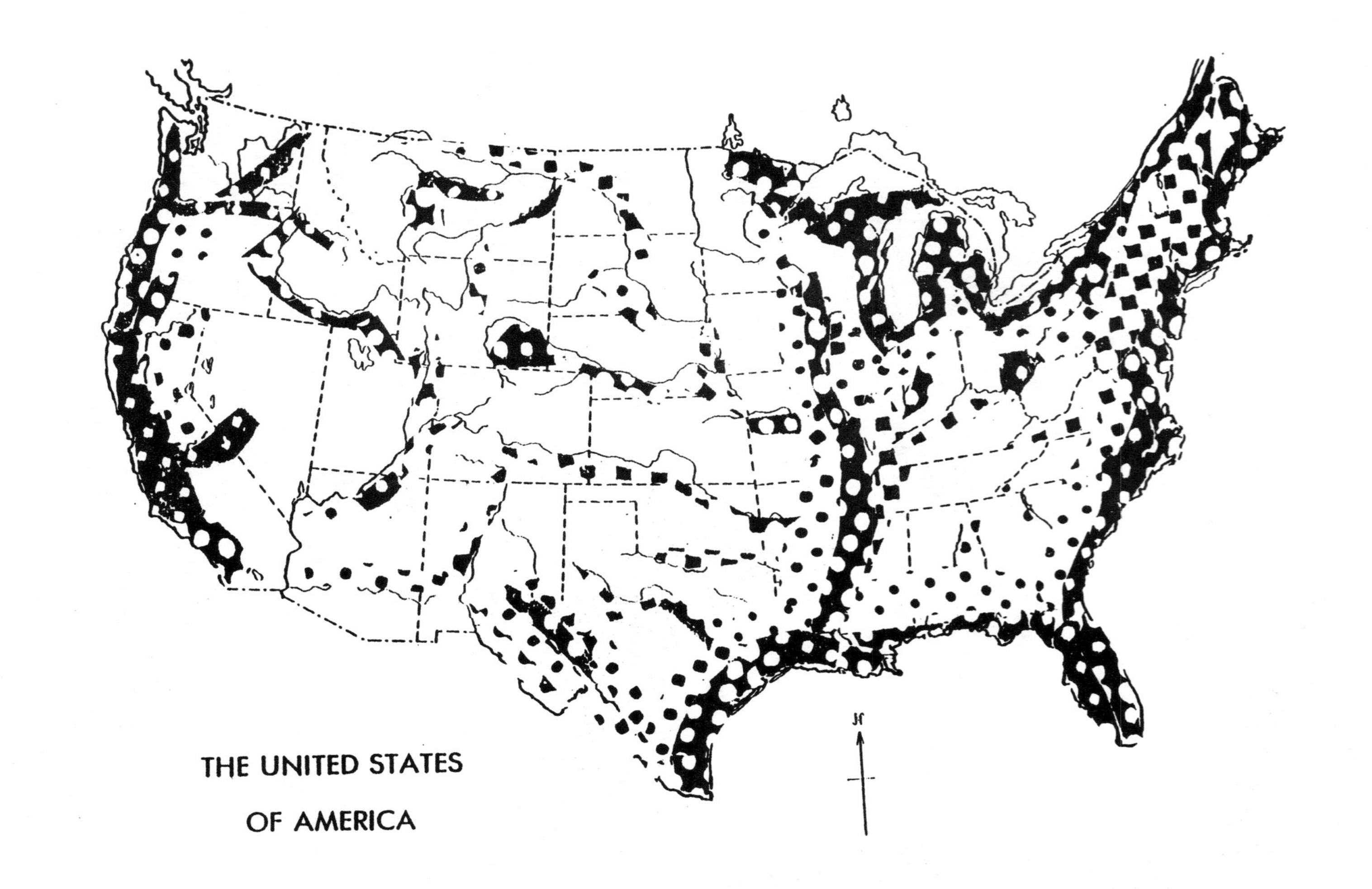

These two maps illustrate a very negative reality which does not need to happen. Potentially, all the land covered by black will be completely underwater. Areas in white will be still be dry land. Areas of white with black dots will be waterlogged and partially flooded. Areas in black on the map on the facing page represent areas that are unliveable due to flooding.

NORTH AMERICA

countries also; sometimes a country which is trying to take-over a disaster-strickened area, will then fall apart itself due to earthquake or other natural disaster.

5. The U.S. political system will be in chaos. Presidents will not be able to serve out their four year terms. The office of the Presidency will become inoperative but the government will try to hide this fact from the people.

The military will be asked to take actions in order to help people caught in natural disasters, but most of the time, the military will be misused, misguided, and ordered wrongly so that the people are not helped. Instead the military will be used in battles of political superiority and dominance. As first one dominant leader, then another, emerge from the chaos, they will attempt to use the military as their own personal pawns.

6. Portions of some U.S. states will be underwater, and as a result, new states will be formed, dividing what is left of the original states. Other states will attempt to leave the union, similar to Civil War days! This chaos will also be hidden from the people; mass media and communication will have broken down, so there will be only word-of-mouth to keep the citizens informed.

7. Billions of people will be driven from their homes. Millions of homes will tumble into earthquake chasms, succumb to tidal waves, volcanic lava, or rock slides, or become permanently submerged under many feet of water. The weather will be severe due to the climate change, so that summers will be hotter and the winters will be harsher.

Billions of people will literally have to return to surviving "the elements," living in what is left of the countryside. Oil and fuel will not be available; not only will transport systems for supplying it have broken down, but in many cases, the land that the oil comes from, will be devastated or underwater.

8. Financial systems will unravel. Currency from a number of former countries will be completely valueless, and even the U.S. Dollar, the German Deutschmark, and the Japanese Yen will be vastly devalued and worthless in some places. "Money" will simply be not-applicable in the life of the common person in the ensuing chaos.

A few extremely wealthy people will try to buy their safety, but there will be few havens which are safe. Also, crowds of angry people will attack the ultra-rich, breaking down their walled and armed fortresses. The common people will feel they have nothing to lose.

Multinational corporations will feel they still exist, but in fact, they will have no financial hold on people anymore. If a flood washes away your home, and the society is so chaotic that you cannot be housed otherwise, you will not care if your credit card is not being kept up to date. In a variety of similar ways, the Earth Change Days will have a silver lining because the multinational corporations and the elite cartels which run the world, will lose their power and their wealth. Eventually, they will cease to exist.

Organized religions will also lose their power base, because society with its proper churches will have fallen apart; also, people will feel alienated from old religious teachings and look directly to the Earth Mother and the Sky Father for inspiration and help. Nature will be the ruling force.

9. We have just mentioned that the sources of oil will in some cases, be no more; those countries will have fallen to ruin in disasters, or be underwater. This also holds true for areas which furnish the world with food and other needed crops.

People will begin growing their own food in small gardens, for their family's use alone. People will fight over usable land, although enlightened people will quickly figure out how to work together with their surviving neighbors for the benefit of both families. Those who are psychically in tune with the Mother Planet will find that growing crops is much easier; they will be able to interpret her moods, knowing when weather will change, and sensing what will grow successfully.

Farming will return to the ancient way, but with modern knowledge applied. A person who is educated in mystical, spiritual wisdom, will work with the land as a shaman, and then modern techniques in crop rotation and fertilizing will be applied as well. Eventually, the best of both worlds will emerge, and this will be part of the bright new dimension which will begin to dawn. This new dimension must be closely linked with the Mother Planet!

10. Cultures will come together which had not been forced to mingle before. Because large areas of some countries will be washed away, nations will find themselves with new neighbors, and they will be forced to work together. Old wars will have to be forgotten. However in some cases, racial groups will still foolishly go to war with their new neighbors because they will view cultural differences as an invasion. In several cases of old wars, when one side is weakened through extreme natural disasters, the other side will attempt to conquer once and for all.

In short, those who are enlightened will find a silver lining to the chaos. Those who cannot change will perish as they attempt to win old wars and conquer new territory; they will attempt to take advantage of weakness but this is, in fact, their weakness! As they attempt to conquer and take advantage, their own undoing will ensue.

The catastrophes will be worldwide and as time goes by, no country or group will be unaffected. If effort and resources are put into the invasion of a neighboring country, weakened by huge natural disasters, the conquering country will find itself in the middle of its own huge natural disaster soon enough, and totally unprepared. Wise leadership will not try to conquer or annex new land, even though that land has been thrown into chaos with no political or governmental system; wise leadership will try to keep its own citizens organized into some kind of responsible tribal unit which can help itself. Ancient times will be happening again!

11. Psychic phenomena will occur with more frequency. This is partially because people will be returning to primitive living and thus have more opportunity to observe the psychic world. Because the psychic world is part of the natural world, you are more likely to see a ghost in a forest than in a modern office building, or at least, you will have the time and be in the mood to observe the forest ghost. Modern life has caused humans to be out-of-touch with themselves. Most people would not see a ghost in a modern office building if it manifested before them; people are involved with the complex artificial world which they themselves have created, and this blocks their psychic sense.

Also, human beings will begin to rebuild their link to the Creator; those who do not will not survive. This link includes the awakening and enhancement of the psychic sense.

Finally, a huge increase in psychic phenomena will be occurring during the Change Times. The Mother Planet is the source of the supernatural as well as the natural; in fact, the supernatural *is* the natural! As Gaia feels angry at what humankind has done to her, her power (which is also her anger), will be unleashed, causing the global catastrophes but also unharnessing psychic manifestations and experiences.

Earth is laced with *ley lines*; these are Gaia's nervous system and they carry psychic energy. The ancients knew about these ley lines and used them for great power. We will devote an entire chapter to *ley lines* but we do predict that they will become much more active and charged as Earth Changes take place. This will lead to amazing psychic experiences and sightings for billions of people. In the middle of the global upheavals, these psychic events will have a profound effect on the human race as a whole.

12. Aliens will land. They will meet humans in great numbers face to face for the first time. Many aliens will offer their starships and their expertise in order to help humanity and other Earth life-forms. These aliens will come from a number of worlds and sources, but most will be positive, loving beings who wish to help. They will help control the few negative aliens who will also emerge from the shadows.

As well as extraterrestrial aliens, humankind will at long last meet other-dimensional beings of Earth in great numbers. With the sweeping Earth Changes, dimensions will have opened up or in some cases, other-dimensional beings will choose to make themselves known and to interact with humanity. As with outer space aliens, most other-dimensional beings have great goodness and wisdom, and humankind will have much to gain by the opening of dimensional doors. Humans who are versed in spiritual metaphysics and who are of good intent, will do well in this new world!

CHAPTER ONE: TIBUS SPEAKS

This is Tibus. I come to you in love and light.

I am honored to be writing this book with Diane. That is, I am telepathically channeling messages to her. A number of other beings wish to communicate with you also, and will be contributors to this book The time is right for us to give you our messages, because the time left within the current Earth reality is very short.

Like water swirling down a drain, time runs faster and faster these days as the daily dimension unravels. There are many natural disasters such as volcanic eruptions, earthquakes, floods, hurricanes, drought, extreme heat, polluted air, and more. This is because of these "Change Times" which spell the end to reality as you know it. Humanity has almost singlehandedly caused these radical times to occur, from the ozone holes in the atmosphere to the barren land where once great rainforests stood.

However, Doomsday need not be a foregone conclusion. Yes, things are falling apart, both in the natural world and in the political/governmental arena, but the human race has the ability to evolve, leaving this "mess" behind! I mean this in a most real and absolute sense, not in some nebulous religious way. A bright, new, real future awaits each and every individual if this spiritual evolutionary leap can be made. And a bright, new, real future awaits the poor bedeviled planet called Earth.

How can this leap be made? Let us help you survive these tumultuous days through using your spiritual and psychic powers; together we can create a new reality; after all, you create your daily reality all the time. Now, you must take control of this ability and stop allowing it to control you. You must *consciously* begin to engineer your new reality.

The bright new dimension of which we speak is still Earth, but it is an *alternate Earth* in which the frequency of being, thinking, and feeling, has risen. The mind waves of this new frequency will be of a higher level. The old "frequency of mind" which encourages greed, cruelty, and insensitivity, will be extinct, unheard of.

If you have made efforts to evolve spiritually, your step upward into this alternate Earth timeline will be a natural and easy one and you will never know at what microsecond it has happened. Your high frequency will match that of the new, risen frequency which is the fabric (the reality) of this New Earth.

What about the Earth left behind? I refer to that Earth and those upon it who refuse to evolve spiritually? In that reality, it is indeed Doomsday.

I am of an Earth which did take that spiritual step in evolution, and so I am willing and able to reach out in Space/Time to help you find that frequency which is enlightened, gentle, peaceful, and just. And I am not alone! At this crisis time in Earth history, there are many angelic, space, and other-dimensional beings who have clustered around Earth to help you, and to help Earth herself.

Artist's rendition of Diane channeling one of her space/dimensional friends. Artist: Merrilie Miller.

Together we offer you this **Bible of Earth Changes**. We also offer to enter your life as active, real spiritual beings, to help protect, guide, and give you new strength.

Will humanity meet space aliens, time travelers, and other-dimensional people soon? Yes, part of being able to evolve spiritually means being able to meet alien beings, face to face, without prejudice or fear. There are beings within your own galaxy whom you can not even begin to imagine, and yet they are highly intelligent and usually peaceful.

Is humanity ready to take its place in the cosmic community of races? My human friends, your survival depends on a "Yes!" answer to that question.

Perhaps you feel discouraged as you realize that humanity cannot even get along with itself, thus there are racial, religious, and cultural wars where one group of human beings seeks to eliminate the other group of human beings. Also, there is racial and religious tension, discrimination, and violence all over the planet. The answer is simple: Those who cannot rise above this level will not be able to survive in the new, risen frequency of mind/soul. The new dimension which results from the Alternate Earth timeline we are helping you create, will be a place where prejudice, cruelty, and violence cannot exist. These will be extinct. Those who live by these dreadful emotions will not be able to take the step upward.

You will find that this survival guide offers help in spiritually surviving and evolving as well as help in physically surviving these Change Times. Many beings offer you this help, just as many beings sent channeled messages of help and deliverance in **The Bible**. Thus we call this guide **The Earth Changes Bible**.

Telepathic channeling is not a new phenomenon, as documented in the Old and New Testaments. Allow this phenomenon to help you now, as your planet faces its gravest crisis.

I have guided, protected, and loved Diane since her birth here on Earth. I met with her in her childhood UFO encounters. I have appeared to her several times in her adult life and I have channeled telepathically to her on a conscious level for fourteen years now. I am proud that we have helped so many people. I am her soulmate, yes, and we share consciousness.

Other enlightened people also feel the presence of a soulmate or star guardian these days; in these critical times, it is urgently important that enlightened humans reach out for conscious contact with us. Each and every one of you has a guardian who will guide you as you join with others on Earth and above, to engineer the risen Alternate Earth. Listen. Learn. Join us!

May the healing light of God and goodness surround you, always,

(I AM Tibus)

CHAPTER TWO: THE REALITY CONTINUUM

No prediction is written in stone, and this includes our "12 Basic Earth Changes."

The future is always an open book; the future can always be created. The future can be engineered to manifest in a particular way but few people realize this, feeling instead that they are trapped in the present and will be trapped in whatever happens in the future as well.

Predictions are really helpmates which are intended to guide you into creating the future in a positive way. In this way, they are wonderful psychic and spiritual gifts but they must not be thought of as paving the way to doomsday or as forecasting negative events over which we have no power. We *do* have power over future events; predictions are partially responsible for giving us this reality-creating power.

Everyone is aware that some psychics have predicted "The Big One" to strike California at this particular time or that particular time. Earthquakes have come and gone, and psychics have come and gone, but still the ultimate "Big One" has not struck! The Big One did not strike on May 8, 1989, for instance; this is one of many dates which have been set by psychic predictions.

Let's look at earthquakes in these Change Times of the last few years of the Twentieth Century; let's consider an Earthquake Continuum which goes from "1" to "10."

At "1" on our continuum, there will be no "Big One" in California, but only the usual series of minor and middle-size quakes such as are bound to happen along fault lines. After all, we cannot pretend The San Andreas Fault is not there, nor, can we ignore the thousands of other faults which run along and through California.

At "2" on our Earthquake Continuum, there are a few more quakes than in years past and several of these are over 6.5 on the Richter Scale. Still, there are no quakes as large as 7.2.

Our continuum progresses through continuum points 3, 4, 5, growing slightly more severe with each number.

"7" on our continuum sees Los Angeles' freeways in ruins and thousands of people killed. Electrical power is lost for days, emergency facilities are overwhelmed with the injured.

"9" on our continuum sees coastal areas underwater after a huge tidal wave, millions of people killed, modern civilization ravaged into nonexistence in a wide area of California.

"10" sees an entire chunk of California fall into the ocean, leaving the Mojave Desert as beach front property. Or perhaps all land west of The Rockies is underwater or, at least, water bound.

A prediction about earthquakes in California might be made which focused at any point on the Earthquake Continuum. It is not a foregone conclusion that "10" will happen, even in these days of Earth's anger, thus increased quake activity.

The psychic/spiritual power of prayer and meditation can make reality less harsh. We have proof that psychic energies do lessen earthquake severity because our **Star Network** of light workers has applied itself to sending calming energies to Mother Earth; we have worked extremely hard on psychically preventing a "10" on the Earthquake Continuum, and a "10" has not happened!

You might say that because a "10" has not happened, it does not mean it will not, or that we prevented it in the first place. This is true. But most Americans believe in the power of prayer and meditation, yet we do not send this spiritual energy to our Mother Planet. For some reason, we of the modern world think we simply cannot "talk" to her!

Why have the predictions of various psychics regarding The Big One been wrong thus far? What has prevented The Big One from happening? "9" has not happened, either, and even a "7" has not quite occurred.

We do know that psychic meditation and prayer helps us all toward a positive reality! And we also know that predictions which have been made forecasting earthquake doomsday have been our helpmates, because they form a point on the continuum from which we can steer away! Reality can be made to go in the opposite, positive direction along its continuum. Predictions of doom and gloom set guideposts. From these markers, we steer toward the light!

Reality itself has a continuum just as earthquake severity can be put on a continuum. Those who study spirituality and metaphysics know this, but many people never realize this truth. They feel that "reality is reality." However, every dimension has a reality base. This is what most people perceive as *the* reality, unchangeable and constant, but it is only the reality in one base of reality.

Connecting the Reality Continuum

Let's consider our Reality Continuum as it connects to upcoming Earth Changes. At "1" on our continuum, there are no more "earth changes" than we are experiencing already. There seems to be a slight global warming with lots of storms and floods, but in a few years, the climate veers back toward being normal. We also experience a few extra hot summers and extra cold winters, but then moderation returns and dominates the climate. The situation with the depletion of the atmosphere gets no worse and millions of new trees are planted; rain forest destruction comes to an end. The ozone holes go away as humankind learns not to use substances which destroy that layer of our protective atmosphere. The layer recovers faster than anyone dreamed possible.

Each intersect point on our Reality Continuum grows more severe and violent. At "7" at least half the polar ice caps have melted, tidal waves have destroyed millions of miles of coastline worldwide, scores of volcanos have come alive after thousands of years of lying dormant, the governments of island nations are falling due to panic in the streets, and Texas and California have left the United States union, forming their own countries.

The 12 Basic Earth Change Predictions which we have just given you, are a "9" on our Reality Continuum. So, you see, these predictions are not written in stone; they are only one possible Reality Base (one point on our continuum).

"10" on this continuum is Doomsday with all life as we know it, ceasing to exist on Planet Earth. The totally melted ice caps cause Earth's axis to become unstable, and the planet breaks into billions of pieces, floating into the oblivion of deep space.

While both science and the psychic world agree that Earth and all her inhabitants are in for some very difficult days ahead, Doomsday ("10") is not a foregone conclusion. "9" is not written in stone, either, and so forth.

Basic metaphysics, which is as ancient as the human race itself, teaches us that we create our reality. We not only *perceive* the reality around us, we *participate* in creating it.

It may be too late to choose a nice, friendly "1" on the Reality Continuum, because already the polar caps have cracked, icebergs many times larger than any before, have sailed into warmer waters for several years in a row. The ozone holes become smaller but then, a new gaping hole opens up the size of Europe, larger than any before. Planting millions of new trees would be grand, but no one is doing this on a large enough scale, rainforests are still being decimated, and besides, how long does it take for new trees to grow large enough to help the carbon dioxide situation?!

Therefore, it is a foregone conclusion that we are in for harsh climate changes, an increase in skin cancer due to the ozone depletion, less pure air, some political upheaval, a partial buckling of financial and governmental systems (we can see this happening even now), and many other drastic changes which we would not have chosen.

But as enlightened human beings, we can spiritually and psychically create/choose a Reality Base which is not total Doomsday and which is not even "9" in terms of utter destruction. We have this spiritual/psychic power within us. This is an invaluable fact to know as you face into the winds of Earth Changes! *This fact in itself is priceless in your own survival!*

To increase spiritual/psychic power, we urge you to become involved with Gaia, the spirit of the Mother Planet. *Become one with her, just as a shaman priest is one with her!*

You do not have to do anything "official" to know her well, simply be yourself and allow her to manifest herself. Allow God to contact you, and allow your God Spark to flow outward. Allow your higher self to shine through, out in Nature's glorious environment.

CHAPTER THREE: WHAT IS AN "ALTERNATE REALITY"?

My star guardian Tibus has long spoken of "alternate realities."

A short definition is simply, "An alternate reality is one of the 10 points along our Reality Continuum."

In one alternate reality, 75% of the ice in the polar ice caps melt, and many other global upheavals become reality.

In another alternate reality, Doomsday strikes Planet Earth, and life is no more.

In yet another alternate reality, all goes along as it is now, and in fact, gets noticeably better in a year or two.

The mind boggling fact is, *you are in an alternate reality right now!* Every branch which reality takes, creates an alternate reality to the path which might-have-been. And that might-have-been path is also an alternate of the one you are in now. It goes on and on, growing more complex, branching into alternate realities which stretch to infinity.

It is not only metaphysics which tells us this (and has for thousands of years), now quantum physics has scientifically proven the same fact about the fabric of Space/Time. Now science tells us the same thing about the nature of reality.

You as a conscious spark can choose your reality! Which branch of reality do you want? Which path will you walk?

How many of us would choose to walk the path which Earth takes into Doomsday? Your mind and soul have the power not to choose that path!

How many of us would choose the alternate reality wherein The Big Earthquake never happens, and only a couple of shakers in the 7.0 range on the Richter Scale rattle California in the last years of the 20th Century? Certainly those of us who live in California would like to find ourselves in this Reality Base!

Since your mind not only perceives the reality around you, but also participates in creating it, you can actively start steering yourself and your loved ones toward a positive alternate reality. You can do this through psychic power, especially if you join with others who are trying to raise the frequency.

By "raise the frequency," we mean that each alternate reality resonates on a particular frequency of consciousness.

If you and other enlightened human beings raise your consciousness to a particular frequency, you will then be within that higher frequency of consciousness. You will have evolved into a new reality!

In fact, that "new reality" is just one of an infinite number of alternate realities, one intersect point on the Reality Continuum.

You will not know the exact microsecond you leave the reality which is headed for Doomsday, and move upward into the reality which is headed for a bright new world, but you can do this!

Look at your own frequency, get in closer touch with your own spirituality. Know your own God Spark within. Know Mother Nature as your friend and companion. Do these things and your spiritual/psychic power will increase tenfold. Your frequency of being, feeling, and thinking will be raised. With these advancements made, you will survive the Earth Changes!

You will be helped in surviving in practical ways, too, once you evolve your spiritual frequency. Better "luck" will be yours and your keen insight and intuition will be invaluable in physically surviving. You can stay ahead of the game, as they say.

As a simple example of this, if you knew how to pitch a tent but did so in a "wash" (dry river bed), you might wake up to find yourself floating down the river after a desert rainstorm! It was important to know literally how to pitch the tent, but even more important to know the secrets of Mother Nature. You should have known not only what a "wash" looks like, but also, you should have been intuitively in tune with nature so that you sensed the infrequent desert rain storm before it struck. Someone who is one with Mother Nature in a psychic sense, would have known these things.

Famous Giant Rock contactee Gabriel Green and Diane getting together to discuss earth changes.

CHAPTER FOUR: SILVER LININGS TO BAD REALITIES

My guide Tibus points to the analogy of a child learning a lesson: If the parent allows a child to trip when he refuses to tie his shoelaces, the child will soon learn the reason for tying them and thereafter, will tie them!

If humankind is allowed to skim by in a pleasant reality, even though they have decimated their planet, will any lesson be learned? Aren't we then just forestalling Doomsday, because it will happen all over again!

If our Reality Continuum by some miracle holds at "1" and the atmosphere clears up, storms and earthquakes dissipate, water levels settle down, and so forth, what will humankind have learned about taking care of their planet and the lifeforms there upon?

In other words, if the parent ties the child's shoes before the child ever trips, the child will never bother to tie his shoes. The parent will always be handy.

Some people say that if advanced beings from space and other dimensions are really here, and people really hear from them through telepathic channeling methods, then these higher beings would certainly stop the disasters which are befalling Earth.

Some people ask, "Why does this space being just channel messages to you, why doesn't he plug up the hole in the ozone if he is so advanced?"

In fact, I did receive a channeling from Tibus which stated that his space people were working to close the holes in the ozone layer. He likened this to patching a tire, stating that even with their advanced technology, they could not fix the entire atmosphere, but that since the holes were getting dangerously large, they would attempt to patch them. Strangely enough, it was shortly thereafter that newspapers worldwide reported the largest of the ozone holes had grown considerably smaller!

Space/dimensional intelligences *do* help us in ways which we usually do not comprehend or are not aware of. But in the "bigger picture" sense, they cannot and will not interfere "from above" and stop us as a human race from learning the sacred lesson of taking care of our home planet!

It is also the lesson of being in spiritual touch with our home planet; this has been completely lost, as we have mentioned. Humankind does not recognize itself as a part of nature anymore; this is a terrible mistake.

Every alternate reality which has a lot of catastrophe and destruction of life as we now know it, also has a shining silver lining. This silver lining is the fact that we survivors of the human race, will have been through so much by the time the Change Times settle down, that we will never make those mistakes again. We will have evolved as a race. Just like the child with his shoe strings, we will know why we must tie our shoes, and we will do so!

So, should we opt for a bad reality so we can learn our lesson?

The answer to this is, "No!"

Strive for the Positive!

We must always strive for the positive. We must always be of good intent. This is a truth which Jesus Christ taught, and teaches still, today.

We must not just sit back and let the worst of all possible realities unfold, or settle for the next to worst of all possible realities.

"Do unto others as you would have them do unto you."

"What goes around, comes around."

There is no other way in which you can raise your own frequency into the shining new world other than to be of good intent, and to try your hardest to make the world a better place.

Most people don't include the fact that they can work *psychically* to make the world a better place, but this is an important power which must be used at this time!

Things are bad enough! It is a foregone conclusion that humankind is about to learn a very rough lesson. There is too much damage already done to the planet for us to escape with a pleasant "1" on the Reality Continuum. We really need to work extremely hard to steer this reality away from Doomsday itself, and onto a less severe alternate reality. From there, we attempt to make the leap in consciousness, into a new risen frequency which heralds a new world, a new reality.

"God helps those who help themselves," and what we are helping ourselves toward, is a brand new dimension!

We will take with us into this new dimension, the beautiful Mother Planet, for she exists in all alternate realities.

Nature is God, and God is Nature. We will take with us, the animals and plants of Earth, because they are in balance with their Mother Planet. Only humankind within this 20th Century Reality, is out of balance.

What better silver lining could there be to these days of frightening Earth Changes? And what more helpful survival plan than to step up the awareness ladder, into a shining new alternate Earth? It is a dimensional step, a step in spiritual evolution, a raising of our frequency, and we as a race can do it!

CHAPTER FIVE: CONTACTING NATURE'S SPIRITS

Diane's Message: Growing up an only child on a farm in Iowa forced me to be very close to nature, because there was no one and nothing else to relate to! But from my earliest recollection, I absolutely adored nature's animals and cherished the land. I loved the trees and would give them individual hugs each day, feeling their life force pounding inside their mighty trunks.

When my family sold our farm in northern Iowa and moved to suburban Florida, I was heartbroken. Surprisingly, this is an emotional scar that has never quite healed despite my many travels in the world.

I firmly believe that had I not been so close to nature, the two UFO "abductions" I experienced in childhood would never have taken place. I put "abductions" in quotation marks because these encounters with Tibus and several of his crewmates aboard their starcraft were completely peaceful and happy experiences. I still feel great joy as I remember these as well as adult encounters I have had with my star guardian Tibus.

However, this book is not being written to document my experiences or my somewhat unorthodox life. It is being written as a detailed guide to help you survive these times of sweeping, sometimes violent change as the Twentieth Century steamrolls to a close.

I have always known that *nature* is the foundation upon which my UFO experiences and psychic talents are built. I communicate telepathically with nature as easily as many people chat with a group of friends. I have healed her animals on many occasions, I can tell the next move of a storm, can interpret the message of the breeze on a hot summer day, and I can tell when a tree is less than healthy. Stray dogs and cats know immediately that I am a true friend. The list is endless, nature is simply an open book to me. I say this in all humility because this is just natural to me, just as playing the piano well is natural to a gifted pianist.

Loving Nature

My ability to telepathically receive Tibus' channeled messages, as well as the transmissions of other space aliens, nature spirits, and other-dimensional Earth beings, is connected to my ability to understand and to consciously be a part of Mother Nature. However, I channeled Tibus for seven years before I began regularly receiving messages from these other entities. Therefore, I was well-prepared by the time I heard from entities such as the volcano goddess, a bizarre alien of the reptile family, an other-dimensional tribe with a mass mind, and more. But always, their messages are sent in love and good faith, and they all relate to helping humankind and Planet Earth survive Doomsday!

How better to be warned that a volcanic chain is coming alive after millions of dormant years, than by the living essence of that volcano chain, the spirit (goddess) of the volcano! And think of the wisdom to be gained if we could communicate with the ancient tribes who built Newgrange in Ireland, or

Stonehenge in England!

They had astounding astronomical knowledge which is not matched even today. They could tell us how to survive Earth's time of upheaval because they understood the secrets of earth and sky.

I realized as I continued channeling these fascinating entities that we do have access to amazing mystical knowledge through the phenomenon of channeling and that these "voices from beyond" can and will give us as human beings the key to surviving our planet's Change Times!

Here, then, is a message I have received from B'Tamei, The Goddess of the Volcano:

This is B'Tamei and I am a Gaian spirit.

("Gaia" is the term used to indicate the living spirit of Planet Earth).

Hello to all receiving this transmission. You may also think of me as a nature spirit. I have been referred to by many names by various segments of the human race for thousands of years, but to make matters clear, you may simply think of me as the Goddess of the Volcano. I am the spirit which drives every volcano!

In Earth's early history, I dominated the reality, creating mountains, valleys, rivers, lakes, and deserts. I helped form entire supercontinents, then watched over their demise as continents drifted, transforming into smaller continents.

Always I have worked closely with the energy-entity who hovers near each and every earthquake, but this entity has not taken form as I have, because earthquakes by definition are spread over and under miles of ground, not harbored and nurtured in a volcanic cone. I have been able to "take form" because volcanoes are "housed." We might compare this to a ghost existing in a theater or hotel. Entities are able to manifest as "beings" perceivable by humankind, when there is a housing around them which can echo the molecules of their consciousness.

I have become famous throughout time, worshipped by the Hawaiians and many other island-dwelling people. They have felt that I dwell in their mountains, inside the volcanic cone, and they have been right! At times I have been seen hovering over the volcanic cone or overseeing the molten lava as it tumbles down the hillside, covering all in its path. There are even photos of me, an awesome female form floating above the smoldering volcano. To be seen and photographed by the human world is to prove to you that not only do I exist, but how powerful and omnipresent I am! Do I sound egotistical?

Perhaps I am, but you must understand that I am an *amoral* entity, as are most Gaian spirits. Humans can be *moral* and do what is right in their perception; sometimes this perception is limited. As an example, I ask you, is the man doing the right thing to jump in the water to save a young boy from drowning? "Yes," you say, but what if I told you that young boy grew up to be Adolph Hitler?

Humankind can also be very *immoral* and I need give you no example of this, because the proof is all around this suffering planet. But me, I am *amoral.* I am not concerned with right or wrong in the human sense. Volcanic activity takes lives and destroys homes. I do not take pleasure in this destruction, it is not the point of my awakening, but neither do I consider the potential harm when my driving force activates yet another volcano.

And in these last days of the Twentieth Century, individual volcanoes and volcanic chains are awakening all over the planet!

Do you think it is time you learned to communicate with me again as the island peoples once did?

Gaia, the spirit of Planet Earth, sometimes comes to me when she is hurt and angry by all that humankind has done to her. It is like your human body turning to its blood pressure mechanism to express anger and stress from within. The hurt and anger must be ventilated somewhere, and your blood pressure rises just as my volcanic driving-force awakens. Earthquake activity works in a similar way.

Perhaps it seems simplistic to you as a modern human that "primitive" islanders offer flowers, fruits, and even blood sacrifices to me in hopes I will become placid and serene. But such people have spiritual wisdom in attempting communication with me!

Have you not heard of a soothing meditation tape to help control your blood pressure? There can be a positive outcome in trying to reach the essence of "me" with calming, reverent offerings which *symbolically* show that I am perceived and respected.

The Planet's Control Mechanism

Because I am a "mechanism" of Gaia when she is hurt and angry, I warn you that I am not automatically a "love and light" being! I like to be worshipped; taking life or causing destruction is neither here nor there to me. When the planet was young, it was a violent place. Land masses rose and fell, great mountains were crushed, boulders were hurled like pebbles, and fire was everywhere. It was glorious! But as the planet became more stable and entered young middle-age, I receded to her bowels, manifesting only occasionally to a mountainside community here or there, so as to keep my spirit alive.

Like Gaia herself, my existence needs to be recognized; I do not demand worship at this point, but I do demand a reflection in the mirror of reality. Modern humanity does not bother to see my reflection, does not take time to perceive me, the living spirit of the volcano.

Now in these final years of the Twentieth Century, I have no choice; I must awaken. And I have! You have merely to read your newspapers.

I have awakened to soak up some of the stress, hurt, and anger which the Mother Planet feels. I am her blood pressure mechanism and she is a living entity!

My awakening is also the physical indication of a sick planet. If you have a negative health condition, your blood pressure may rise as a symptom of that condition. So it is with Earth. She is ill, thanks to the "most intelligent" animals on her surface. Her middle-aged years have been ruined, her serenity gone. Her good health was her clear, unpolluted skies and her rich green rainforests. Now, they are gravely threatened. No longer can she guarantee that she will give protection and shelter to her wild animals, no longer can she continue to be life-giver to billions of lifeforms.

I, B'Tamei, am angry on her behalf. My consciousness perceives what is happening as well as Gaia's direct messages of internal stress and anger. I must once again manifest with all the ferocious power I can summon. Unlike humankind, I do realize that the fate of my Mother Planet is also my own fate.

I beg you to perceive me in the mirror of reality and to communicate with me and with other nature spirits. This will help save *you* as well as your planet. Telepathy travels instantaneously, you need not live near a volcano or by an earthquake fault line. Recognize our existence. Help us handle the anger which we are inheriting from Mother Earth.

We have no wish to destroy human or other life. And we have no wish to destroy the planet because she is our mother. But the anger and the pressure is very great. Volcanic activity increases, intensity mounts. And I can tell you that this is just the beginning.

I AM B'Tamei.

An Afterthought by Diane

So many times as I carry forth my channeling work, I receive the message that the first thing a person has to do to survive the coming Earth Changes is to consciously recognize his or her link to nature.

After all, nature is God's creative power, manifested within Earth's atmosphere. *We are all natural creatures!* Humans forget this important truth as they go around technically developing the world, spreading cement for parking lots and making atomic bombs.

We can no longer ignore the God Spark within each and every one of us which gives us *life.* We must embrace this natural God Spark *now!* We are all a fragment of God's consciousness, a molecule of cosmic consciousness set down on Planet Earth for a brief while.

It may sound foolish to contact the spirit of the volcano or to hug a tree or to see if a nature spirit can be detected and contacted out in the forest, but these are exactly the kinds of things we should be doing to get in touch with God's true world and to thus get in touch with our own inner God Spark. This we need to do, to survive.

CHAPTER SIX: SURVIVING NATURE'S WRATH, THE PRACTICAL SIDE

We humans are spiritual, emotional, mental, and physical beings. All of these aspects reflect the fact we are part of nature. We need to embrace nature spiritually and emotionally as the last chapter discusses. But we also need to embrace nature mentally and physically.

Why? Because following Earth Changes, the world of factories, stores, highways, currency, and high technology which humans have created, will have crumbled. It will be no more! There will be nothing left but *nature* in many areas of the world.

This nature will be angry, still reeling from the affects of global warming and ozone depletion, still in a state of upheaval and devastation.

Survivors will have to keep themselves and their families alive in this frightening new world. But there is always hope, because after this phase of struggling to survive in the wildest of nature, some will begin to flourish. Those who flourish will be those who know nature best! A new way of feeling, thinking, and being will come into being which reflects natural and beautiful cosmic consciousness, a risen frequency!

We urge you, therefore, to read up on nature's ways and on survival but we especially ask you to *experience* nature in these days before The Big Change.

There are many books written on survival in nature, how to build shelter from materials at hand, how to find food, what plants are edible, how to avoid dangerous insects or reptiles, how to find the warmest spot in the wilderness (or coolest if you are in the super-heated desert), how to find and purify water, and so forth. We will not attempt here to write a detailed guide on these physical aspects of survival; we have too many other vital subjects to cover which have not been written about in other books.

What we are doing is urging you to study the detailed physical aspects of surviving out in nature.

Most important, go experience it as often as possible these days! Go camping. Take long hikes. Simply sit down and commune with nature even in your own back yard. Just this action helps you to listen to nature, to perceive nature, to sense nature, to know nature in a way that most humans have long ago forgotten.

All that we will have left is the remnants of this planet, the tag ends of nature as she was, before the storms, before the rising water, before the ozone depletion, before the volcanic awakening and the earthquakes. However, nature will still be with us!

What will not be with us much longer are all the comforts of civilization as we know it. So, although we are not spending pages on details of how to survive physically in nature under adverse conditions, we cannot stress enough how important it is for you to have this knowledge.

Lead With the Spirit

If an individual is at odds emotionally and psychically with nature, no amount of practical knowledge or camping experience will help him or her survive. Native Americans and Aboriginal Australians long ago incorporated emotional, psychic, and spiritual knowledge of nature into their mental and physical knowledge.

In fact, they lead with their spiritual connection to nature and follow it up with practical (physical) knowledge. We of the "civilized" world tend to think we must have practical knowledge and we completely ignore the spiritual connection we should have to Mother Nature.

We will devote much effort in this book in helping you to establish that *spiritual link* to nature because it is much more difficult to possess. And, as the Native Americans and Aboriginal peoples would agree, it is really the most important knowledge you can have when dealing with nature.

A shaman is in balance with nature; he or she is a conscious part of nature. This is as it should be for all of us, not just the holy people. Nature's mystical secrets unfold before us, great psychic power becomes ours automatically, spiritual wisdom guides our every step, once there is *balance* with nature.

Lead with the spirit, follow it up with practical knowledge!

There is, of course, a bridge between the practical and the spiritual. They should not be in contradiction but should compliment and enhance each other. For instance, if I see an eagle while I am trying to survive on a rugged, remote mountainside, modern society might tell me to ignore that eagle and continue my search for water.

However, if I am lead by my spirit, I might stop a moment to be honored that Sister Eagle had flown low over my head. I would take note of which direction she flew, to feel a blessing from the South Wind or the Western Sunset. I would intuitively then go in that direction, thanking her for her help.

On a practical basis, that eagle might well be headed for the water in a hidden lake, and so taking note of which direction she flew, and following her, might well lead me to water. The spiritual and the practical are not in contradiction, it is not "silly" to perceive the eagle spiritually.

My star guardian and friend Tibus has told me, "On up the road of human evolution, the practical and the spiritual meet and become one. The mystical and the scientific meet and become one. There is no need for conflict between science and mysticism. Or between logic and the psychic world. All are one!"

Tibus continues, "It is only that the human brain, in the late Twentieth Century, has not yet activated 'the bridge' between right and left brain. Once this bridge is activated, the *whole mind* will govern humanity's actions and feelings. And the *whole mind* does not say that one side of the brain has to be right (the practical way), while the other side of the brain is wrong (the mystical way).

The right and left brain are in fact just two different receptors for perceiving the universe. They are perceiving the same phenomena and they will one day compliment each other. Together they will create a vast and wondrous new perception of the universe which humans have not dreamed possible! These two halves come together to create a perception and a world which is much greater than the sum of their two separate parts. A new dimension opens, the frequency has risen!

Artist's rendering of B'Tamei, a volcano goddess.
Artist: Patricia A. Davey

CHAPTER SEVEN: THE SPECIAL POWER PLACE IN NATURE

As you take walks in nature, sharpen your intuitive and psychic skills by seeing if you can sense a place where nature's voice speaks extra clearly.

Since "Gaia" is the spirit and emotional persona of the planet, we might say, see if you can sense where "Gaia" speaks to you in a conscious, powerful and mesmerizing way.

You might be able to feel the presence of a nature spirit in this special power spot; you expect a fairy, sprite or elf to pop out at you. And if you look sensitively enough, you might find an unusual stone, a feather, a sprig of bright berries, or some "proof" that indeed a nature spirit has left you a gift, a teleport from his or her home dimension.

I have "proof" in quotation marks because it is easy to slip into a practical frame of mind. We know that in the practical sense, an unusual stone is not proof that an elf is perceiving you from his other dimensional vantage point. A feather is not proof that a natural entity wishes to interact with you, the human. But now we are thinking with one side of the brain, with the side which analyzes scientifically and tends to negate entire worlds and dimensions because "They don't fit, they aren't logical."

However, we have decided that if we are to survive global changes, we must use our spirit also. We must allow intuition and spirituality to lead the way, then apply science and practicality to help us toward our goal.

Just as we perceived the eagle in the spiritual sense, so we can perceive these teleports from nature spirits. This unusual stone, this sprig of berries, this feather, *is* proof of interaction with a nature spirit in the spiritual reality!

Look for the odd synchronicity, perhaps just this morning you were thinking about a sprig of berries to decorate with. Look for the ingenious symbol, perhaps you saved a small bird from a cat this morning, and now you find a feather right on your path which symbolically says, "Thank you for saving my life."

This is exactly the sense which we need to sharpen! The spiritual/psychic gift has laid dormant too long in humanity. Your *special power place* out in nature can and will awaken this precious gift within you. This spiritual sense more than any other aspect of you, is your God Spark, your portion of The Creator's Consciousness!

Choose your *special power place* as far out in nature as you can to go. If you are handicapped, elderly, or cannot travel easily to the countryside, then you can still sharpen your spiritual/psychic sense by choosing a favorite area of your own back yard or nearby park. If you are active and well, head for the wilderness because nature has more power remaining where humans are nowhere around. However, if you wish to return to your power place for frequent communication and interaction with nature, then choose a place which is accessible and which you don't need an infrequent two week vacation to get to.

Of course you can sense more than one power spot in various natural settings, but do pick one as your "most special" because this is a decisive step to take psychically.

This actively opens the link between you and Gaia.

Transform Your Life

You will be absolutely amazed at how your life will be transformed, once this link to Gaia, the soul of our planet, opens! This soul has been ignored throughout the dark days of organized religion when humanity was taught to look only to the skies for male deities in human form. God. Allah.

We do not say that these male deities in the heavens are not valid. But the Mother Planet is also a valid creator, a very real and powerful entity. A Goddess.

The Creator certainly has a male aspect and a female aspect. How else does the miracle of creation happen? The two genders are a universal constant. The universe is The Creator's baby, The Creator's work of art. This Creator Spirit is charged with Male Energy and with Female Energy.

Many people accept this Yin/Yang concept but when it comes to perceiving the Female Creator closest to them personally, they turn their backs on the concept. The Female Creator closest to every human is the Mother Planet! It is She who created us and every living thing we know. Why is Her Holy Spirit ignored, then, by modern humanity?

To acknowledge Her and learn to communicate with Her does not negate or detract from our Cosmic Father who is the Male Creator. In fact, to consciously contact Her, enhances His presence in our life.

And, our Mother Planet is so accessible to us, She is everywhere! That is, She is everywhere unless She has been destroyed to make way for a parking lot, a high-rise building, or a super highway. However, it is absolutely guaranteed that every time you communicate with Her, whether on a walk or just gazing at the beautiful rose bush in your yard, you will feel healing energy rush into you. Renewal!

She *is* magic. So don't just admire the rose bush, really *work* on contacting Gaia, who is the living Goddess of the Planet. Offer Her communication. Offer Her respect and love.

Offer Her healing, because the planet is dying.

She always offers healing to Her myriad of life-forms. She always offers life to all Her children. Now we must work very hard on healing Her. We must give Her the will to live. We must hear Her cry and perceive Her tears. Humankind has decimated Her across the globe in more ways than can be listed. One act of destruction leads to many others, because Hers are delicate ecosystems which depend on each other.

We can well substitute "Him" where we have written "Her" because to ignore the dying planet is to ignore God.

We will not survive without our planet. We will be dead, cast to oblivion. And God will be dead.

We wish to note here that we have been capitalizing "She" and "Her" in the above paragraphs. In the interest of simplicity, we will not do this throughout the entire book, but we do feel it is important to acknowledge the Female God as well as the Male.

We cannot urge you enough to find that *special power place* out in nature, that place which seems as though it may be an energy vortex or wellspring of nature's creative energy. Find a place where you can almost hear Gaia's voice. See if you can hear her message, too. You might be surprised at how plainly she speaks. Or, if she herself does not speak, one of her nature spirits may communicate. Or The Oak. Or perhaps The Eagle will deliver her message! Whatever the message or the messenger, Gaia will find it easier to reach you in this power place, and you will find it easier to perceive her! To *feel* Her. To know without a shadow of a doubt that you are a part of Her!

Thus begins a step toward the risen Alternate Earth. Dimensional doors open which you will one day step through, along with the rest of the human race that has managed to achieve enlightenment. The frequency of Earth inches upward.

You will never be the same again. Never so insensitive to the Mother Planet. Never again so psychically blind. Never again to be without the wisdom which the shaman has learned. Never again to be detached from the Creator Spirit. Now this Spirit begins to glow from within, empowering you; and from without, She smiles.

CHAPTER EIGHT: HOW WILL SPACE/DIMENSIONAL BEINGS HELP US SURVIVE, AND WHO ARE THEY, ANYWAY?

A lot of channeled material deals with specific alien races. The Pleiadeans, the Orions, the Draconians, the list is endless as the wealth of channeled material grows. Telepathic channeling is certainly a phenomenon of the late 20th Century. Not since biblical times has this psychic phenomenon occurred in such abundance.

I have channeled my star guardian Tibus since 1982. That is, I began channeling him consciously in that year. But he had always been with me as a spiritual presence, an unseen friend. Four years before 1982, I had begun discovering my "star path." I explored and experienced, trying to find out what I was feeling psychically and spiritually, why I was so obsessed with UFOs and other dimensions. Every individual seeking enlightenment goes through this "time of awakening." It is really an exciting and profound milestone along one's life path; thereafter, life settles down a bit and one begins helping others with counseling, healing, teaching, whatever is needed and whatever your particular spiritual gift is.

"My" Tibus has never said he was from a far distant planet circling a far distant star. He has traveled to these. I am reminded of James T. Kirk in the Star Trek IV film, The Journey Home, when he tells a confused 20th Century human, "I work in space but I'm from Iowa."

When Tibus refers to "space and other dimensional intelligences," one of those "other dimensions" he is referring to, is the dimension of Time. To say that he is a time traveler is perhaps too stereotyped or simplistic, but essentially, that's what he is. He is a Future Human, slightly different than 20th Century humans both in physical genetics and spiritual genetics.

When I remember what he looked like in my childhood encounters with him, he seems "enhanced" or "magnified" beyond what human beings are presently.

This empowerment is physical, mental, and spiritual. Humans from his time/dimension are more psychically gifted than we are; the psychic gift which God/Goddess gave to all of us, has been developed and embraced within his people.

It makes perfect sense to say that this man I met aboard a UFO in my childhood came from a people who had made the leap in consciousness we are taking about in this book. He seems one step more evolved in every way than human beings of the 20th Century. Yet, as a small child, I couldn't put this into words or even into concept. I simply knew that I liked his spiritual vibrations and was not afraid. And his image has stayed with me always, even if in my subconscious for part of my life.

I feel that many people who feel contact with someone "beyond" these days, should look into the possibility that the contact is with a Future Human or similar other-dimensional race. This possibility isn't considered very often.

Like so much else on this crazy star path I have traveled for years now, the childhood contact with Tibus, and his source/identity, all comes together and makes sense, now that I have the mental and spiritual answers. Now I can put it into words! It is extremely inspiring to me that there *are* answers which manifest eventually. It illustrates to me that there *is* a wise and beneficial plan, which will help the planet, and also individuals including myself.

Another example of Tibus and his co-workers having a plan for me which I became aware of years later, is when I began my newsletter, **The Star Network Heartline** in 1983. I am very proud of the fact that this newsletter has not missed a month since its birth, despite the fact I have moved to Amsterdam, The Netherlands, then to the Republic of Ireland, and finally, back to Joshua Tree, California. We have a wonderful group of devoted readers/friends who have loyally followed us around the world via the mail. To them, we are eternally grateful. But, when I began **The Heartline** in Poway, California, I was not sure why exactly I was doing this!

Tibus told me to call it **The Star Network Heartline** and although it was a nice title, I didn't catch the full significance of it then. Nor did I realize how beautifully powerful our **Star Network** was to become in the psychic/spiritual sense of working toward the best of alternate realities! We are now a meditative network of enlightened people who join together at specified times to *raise the frequency.* We are helping to engineer the bright new dimension, and to keep the destruction and suffering to a minimum as the old dimension fades away.

But I did not realize all this in 1983. However, Tibus did! This in itself is startling proof of our star guardians' love for us. There *is* a plan of (positive) alien help.

There have been many other examples in my light work throughout the years which illustrate in a "horse before the cart" way, that I have taken an action or put forth information which much later makes sense and proves there is a plan in motion! It is then that I shake my head in amazement and say, "Tibus, I guess you knew what you were doing all along!"

Tibus has lived parallel aspects (past lifetimes) on alien planets. So have most of the people reading this book. However, his people are Future Humans (we might even call them "super humans"), who were wise enough not to blow themselves up, wise enough not to destroy their Mother Planet, wise enough to treasure the life forms which abound on Earth and throughout the universe. Tibus' people are humans who have taken their place in the galactic community and are respected, proud, and much loved as a (human) species.

This is what we as humans must do: We must become *cosmic citizens.* No longer can we cling to old tribal identities which cause wars, racial hatred, religious bigotry, and cruelty to others because they are not "like" us.

I do not aim to take away from any alien channeling source (that is, channeling from an alien from a far distant planet), but I do feel that Tibus and other Future Humans have their place as wise big brothers and sisters who truly understand us as a species. Tibus is one of us but he has found that alternate reality door which led to a beautiful new dimension. He simply wants to help us find that door as well.

We feel it is a mistake within New Age circles to automatically have great esteem for an alien who comes from far away, but to look down on anyone or anything "earthy." I have heard New Agers say, "Oh, that is such an earthy entity." The implication is that this is not a wise source, this is not a highly evolved being.

We must analyze what each source says, whether he or she be alien or "earthy." Does the message ring true in our heart and soul? Is there undue egotism involved, such as announcing that the only way to spiritual fulfillment is "my way?" Does the message have universal logic? Or is it off the wall? Is the message of good intent or does it put down other people and messages without logical reason?

Connecting Our Alien Links

The truth is, we all have a bit of alien in us spiritually! Some of us have closer extraterrestrial ties than others. Those who seek enlightenment are almost always very ancient souls who have lived lifetimes on far distant planets as well as in ancient times on Earth. But it is easy to get caught up feeling we are from an alien race directly and lose sight of our mission here on Earth: to help save this beautiful blue/green planet, and ourselves. Certainly our goal is more important than to linger too long contemplating our individual cosmic "fact sheet."

If you are from the most highly exalted race in the galaxy, but you do nothing to help raise the frequency on Earth here and now, how can you be so sure you are of that high race? In other words, do you truly act extremely advanced or do you point your finger at those you feel to be of "inferior" or "negative" sources? Isn't this just the old Earth habit of prejudice toward those who are not like you, raising its ugly head again?

Is there really a point in telling the world how wonderfully evolved your people are? Egotism of a typically human source has a way of sneaking in when we least expect it.

I have learned over the years to treasure those who try to *do* something to help, regardless of their source, rather than those who announce up front what planet they are from and how great it is there.

Tibus also has always put stress on *doing.* He says that humans do not realize there is *psychic activism* as well as physical activism. We very much admire the Greenpeace volunteers who put their bodies in front of the whaling ships. That is physical activism! But most of us are too busy struggling with life itself to go out in a Greenpeace boat. However, we *can* be psychically active and spiritually militant. In fact we call ourselves *spiritual warriors.*

Our **Star Network** has Cleansing/Healing Days every month in which we are psychically active, spiritually militant. We are spiritual warriors joined together in heart and soul, all across the globe, with our energies aimed toward healing the planet and helping all life forms who need help.

Our friends of Space/Dimensional Intelligence join with us telepathically on these Cleansing/Healing Days; this is a true joining of human and alien. In fact, this is the first time such an on-going psychic effort has taken place! And we have had very positive results and have seen our psychic power grow.

Amongst our friends of Space/Dimensional Intelligence are extraterrestrials from far distant planets. Most of them have lived a human lifetime or two. Otherwise, we humans would be so strange to them that they could not work with us or our planet. There is a saying, "You cannot imagine what you cannot imagine." There has to be some reference point for an alien to work successfully with Earth and her lifeforms, and particularly, with humans.

Extraterrestrials As Humans

Does it seem odd that an extraterrestrial has lived as a human in a past life? We must realize that things go both ways, because after all, more and more humans are discovering their alien roots and spiritual ties.

I receive many questions asking if Tibus belongs to the Ashtar Command. This group is certainly influential among the Space/Dimensional Intelligence visiting Earth currently in order to help the planet through her Change Times.

Tibus works with The Ashtar Command but he is not directly *of* it. This is true of many alien contacts which people feel. The Ashtar Command is well known, but you need not feel your telepathic alien friend "must" belong to it in order to be one of the good guys!

The important thing is that a vast array of aliens and dimensional individuals have gathered around Earth at this particular time in order to help the planet survive. They do not want us to perish!

They began gathering in the current modern era in 1947, so it is no wonder that this is the year in which the first "flying saucers" were spotted by Kenneth Arnold. It is no coincidence that this was also a time of intense interest in atomic weapons by Earth governments.

Aliens and dimensional beings view atomic energy in a completely negative way and they flock to any planet which is foolishly experimenting or using atomic weapons and energy. This is a matter of galactic concern because a serious thermonuclear war on Earth can cause misalignment to other planets and to other dimensions. Humans do not realize that the Solar System and even the entire galaxy are ecosystems which are co-dependent on each other.

When we ask, "What groups of aliens are on Earth and above Earth in order to help us in these Change Times?" We might more accurately ask, "What aliens are *not* here?!" There is a huge number of extraterrestrial races currently in contact with Earth. We feel less emphasis should be placed on whether this group or that group is "the most advanced" or "the most good." More emphasis must be placed on saving the planet, which is what any group of good intent is here for in the first place!

Other Dimensional Races Come to Earth

Also, there is a huge number of other dimensional (Earth) races currently contacting humans. These include Tibus' Future Humans but also, there are mystical ancient tribes who have never really left the face of Earth. They simply turned "sideways to the sun" as an Irish song says; these ancient races left three dimensional Earth but remained with us in other dimensions.

In future chapters, we will have urgent channeled messages from several of these other dimensional groups. At present, we simply wish to stress that they are an important part of the Space/Dimensional Intelligence who are working to save Earth. A large part of that work is done through making contacts with humans, like you.

Also included in other dimensional groups are the nature spirits which we have already mentioned. These range from fairies and elementals to the Goddess of the Volcano. There is some overlapping here because fairies are also representatives of a mystical, ancient tribe who journeyed into another dimension when they became disgusted with the human race.

Many people are surprised to learn that a group within the positive Space/Dimensional Intelligence who are helping us, are souls who have recently passed on from the Earth plane. These souls have gone onward to New Life and now work from an angelic dimension to help us back here. Obviously when Adolph Hitler died, he did not go to this angelic dimension. This group is composed of humans who achieved great enlightenment and wisdom when alive and who were of pure, good intent.

If you feel psychic contact with your Aunt Sarah who was a remarkable, enlightened woman, kind to children and animals, and who steadfastly believed in life "out there" in the universe despite pressures to be more conforming, it is likely that Aunt Sarah is indeed contacting you from the angelic realm of the Space/Time Intelligence. She is also actively working to save this planet and part of her Assignment: Earth is to telepathically contact others who feel the same. She *knows* you feel as she does, because you and she were always close and viewed life in a similar mystical, positive manner. And, she loves you.

In no way is the traditional Spirit World left out of the current phenomenon which is occurring during these Earth Changes!

In a future chapter, we will give more details on this.

Angels Are Here!

There is also the more traditional Angelic World involved in the Space/Time Intelligence who work with us. This world includes highly advanced archangels such as Michael, with whom a number of light workers feel contact, and also "personal angels" who protect and guide individuals. If Tibus were an angel, he would be my "personal guardian angel."

Tibus smiles at this saying, "I am no angel, I am a 'star guardian.' I am a traveler in time and am not technically an angel. Therefore I am more accurately a *star* guardian. But the concepts of 'star guardian' and 'guardian angel' are very similar."

Also working with Space/Time Intelligence are exalted masters such as St. Germain, Nostradamus, and a number of far Eastern masters. Not all of these masters are well known by name, many did not choose fame or lived hundreds or even thousands of years ago; their memory is lost to the mass human consciousness. Still, these men and women are highly advanced beings and have much help to offer us. The contact you feel may be a "knock on the door" from one of these souls.

We also include on a "last but not least" basis, magnificent Earth prophets and messiahs such a Jesus Christ, Mohammed, Confucius, and Krishna.

The New Age varies in the degree of emphasis placed on Jesus Christ. Many people channel Him as Sananda, from aboard a starcraft.

Others prefer to keep Him as Jesus, the Christ, whom the Bible tells us about, and whom we feel in our hearts.

Still others view Jesus as a remarkable and advanced human being, perhaps even a "super human" from the future. But these people do not view him as a deity or as the ultimate Messiah.

The New Age and the Risen Frequency for which we strive, must be about *tolerance.* All perspectives on Jesus Christ are correct; that is, they are correct within the heart of the person doing the perceiving. This is as it should be.

We have now covered in brief, "*Who are the Space/Dimensional beings who are helping us?*" There will be more information on each of the groups mentioned later in the book.

But we have yet to deal with:

How Will They Help Us In These Change Times?

Star Trek speaks about the Prime Directive of Noninterference. Like so much of Star Trek this concept is an inspired one. Star Trek abounds in implanted visions and we can only wonder if its creator, Gene Roddenberry, had a telepathic conduit to our friends in Space/Time Intelligence.

This noninterference directive states that visitors from outside the present Earth timeline must not interfere with Earth history. This applies to the angelic realms and other dimensional Earth realms as well as applying to extraterrestrials and to future humans. Remember how Captain Kirk and his crewmates could not change history when they traveled back to the 1930s? This scenario is a bit simplistic but it gets the idea across!

Tibus tells me that "purists" within his group argue that the Space/Time Intelligence has already stepped over the line and is interfering too much in Earth's timeline with all the psychic channeling, encounters, UFO sightings, and cosmic contacts which are now happening to humankind.

However, most of our Space/Intelligence friends feel that something drastic must be done in order to save Earth and her inhabitants, and so channeled messages, UFO encounters, and other dimensional psychic contacts continue at full steam. And it is argued that there has *always* been spiritual "interference (input) to the human race from outside.

But when the question is asked, "How are our friends helping us?" we can reply that they *cannot* help us by directly "beaming down" to save us and set everything right again through their high technology and by *forcing* higher awareness. This would be gross interference and "the child" would not learn his lesson.

Human history must be allowed to unfold as humans cause it to unfold.

Besides, can consciousness be higher when it is forced?

If you land in your starcraft and practice mind control over a quarrelling bunch of humans, are you accomplishing anything? And aren't you very wrong to force them to think a certain way, even if that way is "Peace!"

Those who are highly telepathic and who have control over their own psychic powers, have a huge responsibility not to misuse these gifts! Interfering in a particular timeline is morally wrong.

We might mention here that the term "timeline" can be interchanged with "alternate reality." Remember our information about intersect points on the Reality Continuum, and how each of these intersect points is in fact a different dimension, a different reality base?

Each Reality Has a Timeline

Each alternate reality has a unique timeline, with events which occur along that timeline both large and small; these form its history. If you come from an outside dimension of Space and/or Time, and change one of those events, you have altered history and reality, present and future.

Our Space/Intelligence friends do save individual lifeforms more often than anyone realizes. We have read about "walk-ins" who were in "fatal" traffic accidents but who managed to survive, except that after their recovery, they are a different, higher soul. They know within themselves that their old soul did leave during the accident but that a more advanced soul walked in.

There are also many incidents where an individual is saved miraculously and is never quite sure *how*. It is a miracle! Some of these "miracles" are brought about through intervention from "outside."

This also applies to lifeforms other than humans. How many times does a sensitive person "get a message" to save a stray dog or cat in this way or that? And how many dying animals have been "beamed up" to starships and saved, especially endangered species? We shall never know, but we receive a spiritual confirmation that it is *many.*

We all have heard of humans who have cancer, then go into a miraculous remission or who "just happened" not to be there when a plane crashed into their bedroom. Outside interference? In some cases, yes. The list is endless.

However, these are all individual cases of benign intervention.

Our alien friends cannot step in and save our planet and all who live on it, in an obvious rescue and rehabilitation effort. The universal noninterference directive prohibits this; the human race must take the step in spiritual decency and evolution on its own!

Understanding Spiritual Interference

Throughout human history, there has been one area where Space/Dimensional Intelligence can "interfere" and that is in the *spiritual area.*

A quick example: Jesus Christ changed human history. Was he a Future Human? Was he an extraterrestrial? Was he Earthly other dimensional? Or, was he simply The Messiah?

Regardless of how you answer these questions, his spiritual influence on this timeline, forever changed it.

Until now we have told you how our Space/Intelligence friends cannot interfere, but now we will illustrate how they are helping!

They channel messages telepathically to a variety of human "receivers" who then spread the universal wisdom and insight received. *This raises the frequency!*

Aliens to this timeline allow their starships (UFOs) to be sighted by millions of people in both the day skies and the night skies. Radar controllers, pilots, doctors, presidents, policemen, and many more; all have seen and then believed.

These sightings might seem like a physical phenomenon, but in fact they are more of a spiritual one. People *believe*. Suddenly, the air traffic controller starts realizing in the heart of his being, that we are not alone in the universe! He feels this because he *knows* what he saw on his radar screen. The policeman starts reading books on Eastern mysticism because he *knows* what he saw in the sky one starry night! The doctor starts looking into past life regression because she *knows* the light being she saw in her bedroom is a soul she knew in a past life! And the President of the United States quietly reads every UFO book he can get his hands on, because he *knows* what he saw, and it stirs his very soul!

The U.S. President Knows!

We realize that many people feel the President of the United States is completely aware of alien visits and that many presidents have met face to face with the aliens (either negative or positive aliens), and that there is cooperation between the highest levels of governments and aliens. We will deal with this question in an upcoming chapter.

Not only are there millions of UFO sightings, there are also millions of UFO encounters of the second and third kind. If the common person is inspired when he or she views a distant zigzagging light in the night sky or a silver daylight disk, we can imagine how entire lifetimes are changed when an actual encounter with UFO occupants occurs!

Encounters of the second kind involve evidence left behind, such as a burn mark on the ground where the starcraft set down, or a "sunburned" face on the observer who watched the craft up close, or a reversal in the magnetics of a car which a UFO flew over. Evidence of this sort leaves a human observer forever wondering; never again can the universe be viewed in the same closed, narrow manner. The conclusion must be, "We are not alone!" *This raises the frequency!*

Encounters of the third kind involve face to face encounters with UFO occupants. Again, there is a negative aspect to this, the abduction scenario, which may involve frightening medical tests on the hapless human. This is a separate subject which we will deal with later.

We feel that too much emphasis has been placed on the negative side of UFO encounters of the third kind. The vast majority of encounters have *not* involved medical probes or other frightening events.

I know from my own experience that scientific UFO study groups would have paid great attention to me if I had said my childhood encounters were frightening and medical in nature. However, when I honestly stated that my memories of my time aboard the craft were very positive and that I had the feeling of being among family and friends, I was tagged as a crazy psychic. In the language of UFO scientific groups, I was then considered a "contactee" who wasn't worth listening to at all.

Still, there are some very valid aspects to my encounters in scientific terms, and I have some impressive documentation. On the other hand, I know that some people who have hysterically reported bad medical experiences might be remembering subliminated molestation by a family member or a similar negative but very human experience. My point in saying this is that I do not feel all encounters which are "love and light" should be laughed at by scientific groups while all encounters which are frightening and negative should be treated as probably true and highly interesting.

Millions Have Had Encounters

Leaving that debate behind, we can conclude that there are literally millions of people who have had positive encounters of the third kind, and that their lives have been changed utterly.

Much of the popularity of the New Age centers around the encounters and experiences people have had. Some have been physical, face to face encounters with aliens or other-dimensional beings. Others have been astral experiences into the angelic realm. Some feel that they have an "alien" connection, and/or memories within their heart and soul of another lifetime. Still others have involved feeling telepathic contact with a presence who is not human, but who is extremely familiar, loving and wise.

The variations on incredible encounters are as endless as the number of people, worldwide, who are experiencing phenomena!

But one thing is certain: *This raises the frequency!*

In summary, the Space/Dimensional Intelligence feels that to inspire the hearts and souls of human beings, is not direct interference. It is inspiration.

How does one define "inspiration" as opposed to "interference?" Our alien friends provide an infinite source of *inspiration* for us in these very troubled times. It is for this reason this book is being written, and it is for this reason you are reading it!

Our friends do not interfere on an obvious basis, although there is more "positive interference" than we possibly realize. "Positive interference" is a difficult commodity to identify. Tibus' favorite example is, "If you have a fender bender in your car, you may be upset. It is a negative experience. But do you stop to consider that this same minor accident could have been a fatal one? Was there positive interference from your guardians above? It is very possible. Before you feel you are not loved or protected, or that your guardians will not interfere on your behalf, consider what might have been! Maybe they did interfere in a positive sense."

Another footnote to "*How do our alien friends help?*"

Space/Dimensional Intelligence friends do not always contact enlightened human beings by landing their spectacular starships in front of them! Your time of awakening in order to be ready for the Change Times, may have a much more subtle approach. Perhaps you "merely" have an intense interest in the UFO subject. Or in general New Age subjects. Or in herbs and healing. Or maybe you saw a ghost last year and have been thoroughly amazed ever since. Our friends can inspire us through a gentle kind of telepathy rather than a Close Encounters of the Third Kind grand finale.

The entire planet is awakening spiritually. In every country, there are people who are seeking enlightenment, who want to help Gaia, the planetary spirit, who feel they may have alien connections, who aspire to be light workers. This is *the answer* as to how our alien friends are helping us survive Earth Changes. The only way to survive is to raise the frequency, and that is exactly what is happening.

These are very exciting times in which to be living! Frightening, yes, as we see the climate change drastically and other unbelievable events become reality. But I rejoice that I am here, at this precise moment in Space/Time!

CHAPTER NINE: SPECIFIC EARTH CHANGE PREDICTIONS AND HOW TO SURVIVE

I would like to share with you several telepathic channelings I have received which will help you survive these Change Times. They will also give you deeper insight into what is really happening. To be forewarned is to be forearmed; the lifting of ignorance as the light of knowledge shines through is in itself *a miracle!*

THE VIRAL THREAT

Our channelings dealing with predictions and prophecies will be divided into a number of subcategories.

The first deals with predictions of "plague and pestilence" which have been "promised" to us in the late 20th Century.

Every source from The Bible to Nostradamus predicts these frightening diseases. And now we see them coming true, with AIDS as the most obvious, but also with new "super strains" of tuberculosis and other bacteria. Perhaps worst of all is The Virus; it is an alien from hell for which medicine has found no vaccine or cure. The Ebola Virus leads the way as one of a myriad of new viruses which are so violent and potent, that virtually no individual has a chance of surviving. Death comes most horribly.

What do our Space/Dimensional friends have to say about all of this? How can we survive as a race and as individuals?

Let's begin with a channeling from Tibus:

This is Tibus. I come to you in love and light.

I wish to discuss the new viruses and how deadly they are, and will be, to humanity. I wish to discuss also how the human race can overcome them with psychic power as well as with scientific innovation. This concept is testimony to the tremendous *power of spiritual awareness.*

I wish to give you an example in relatively recent human history of the *power of spiritual awareness.* If you wish, you may substitute "the power of spiritual awareness" with "*the power of the human mind*".

In particular, I am addressing the power of the human mind over the microscopic world of (harmful) bacteria and virus.

Let's turn our attention to tuberculosis. It has been around, plaguing humankind, for thousands of years. Graves in Germany dating back ten thousand years, and the Old Kingdom within Egyptian history, give skeletal evidence that people died of TB even then. In Egypt, it is also recorded in hieroglyphic record.

In the Fifth Century, B.C., Greece was ravaged by TB. In ancient India and China, millions died of it. By 1870, it was the dreaded killer of millions in Europe, Canada, and the U.S. In fact, it was all over the planet.

Then something strange happened! There was a sudden, marked and inexplicable decline in TB everywhere that records were kept. But it began, it seems, in Germany in 1882.

There are many scientific possibilities which would explain this partially, though not totally. One is that perhaps TB is self-limiting; that is, it has a kind of population control like most species of animals place upon themselves. If there are too many of one kind of animal, that animal stops breeding as much. Or, disease or disaster wipes out some of them, courtesy of the overseer, Mother Earth. Or, perhaps the human population built up an overnight immunity, but it cannot be said that surgical or chemical innovations helped, because these did not come into existence until after 1900.

From our overview, we star guardians know that the factors mentioned above did play a slight part in checking the spread of TB which had, up to this time, spread wildly along, completely out of control. But we also know the main factor in the dramatic fall of this disease. Allow me to explain it to you now, because this knowledge will help in your survival in the coming Earth Changes.

In 1882, the same year as TB decreased so dramatically in Germany, a German doctor named Robert Koch, described the bacillus Mycobacterium tuberculosis. Dr. Koch later received the Nobel Prize because he not only described the TB bacteria, he also helped in identifying the bacteria responsible for anthrax, cholera, bubonic plague, and sleeping sickness.

But our point here is, that Dr. Koch *only identified the bacteria.* He did not find a cure. He did not find a way to "interact" with the TB bacteria; he did not know how to affect it or its reproductive cycle. He "merely" identified it.

Overcome Fear!

Mycobacterium tuberculosis came out of the darkness! Its cover was blown! It was no longer mysterious. The *fear factor* had been removed (humans fear what is *unknown* most of all). It was no longer the unseen, all-powerful enemy, but merely an identifiable bit of protoplasm, just like all other life.

Yes, it could cause damage and death, but the human race now had within its mass consciousness, the enlightened information on what needed to be fought. The physical body in harmony with the mind/soul, then began to fight the bacteria much more effectively.

Presently viruses are "the great unknown" for the human race, the dark enemy who inspires fear. Remember that in the psychic world, *fear is the most negative force there is.*

In fact, the new super strain of TB has joined with The Virus (as have other bacteria), and is now hiding behind another veil of mysterious darkness. TB has resurfaced because people have let down their spiritual guard concerning it; it seemed no longer to be a threat. TB has again removed itself from the light, thanks to another feared enemy of the human race, The Virus.

But when light is shed on The Virus, it, too, will lose its all-powerful grip. AIDS will no longer be deadly; there will be an intelligent, logical way of fighting it.

It all has to do with the power of the human mind, with spiritual awareness, with the psychic strength of the mass human consciousness. These will overcome (as they have in the past), the terrible dark fear which gives power to the plagues of humankind.

Remember this as the days grow darker, my friend. This is an important part of your personal survival, just as it is an important part of your human race's survival. You can and will emerge into a new and better dimension!

May the healing light of God and goodness surround you, always,

Tibus

Here is another inspiring supplment to the previous channeling:

This is Tibus. I come to you in love and light.

Hello, my co-workers on Earth! Your spiritual strength, wisdom, and understanding will help get you through these final years of the 20th Century. You will need to rely on these gifts more and more. People without this spiritual aspect will find themselves in very serious trouble, feeling utterly lost, thrashing in the deep waters. Survival itself will become difficult.

It is dawning on a growing number of people that Planet Earth's immune system is badly weakened. This is the short answer as to why humans suffer with AIDS, sea mammals suffer from immune deficiency illnesses, primates suffer from their own immune weakening, and the list grows longer of species becoming immune-weakened.

Don't humans realize that every life form is linked to the Mother Planet so closely that if her immune system is weakened, theirs is, too?

To say that Earth has AIDS is a bit simplistic but it is basically accurate. I hasten to add that this planetary disease can be cured, or if not precisely cured, then the planet can be eased through the crisis. Then, because she is such a strong creative force, she can recover slowly but surely.

But it will take much brave work on the part of spiritual and environmental activists. And it will take nothing short of a leap in consciousness into a new, higher frequency. It will take a dimensional change! There is no alternative, but happily, the change is a joyous and positive one. A wondrous bonus!

Finally, I have to grin at the recent discovery of "the dinosaur sitting on her eggs" in the Gobi Desert. Why oh why do humans always assume that they are the only species who loves its young? It is the same kind of conceited conclusion which has made humans think for centuries that dinosaurs were cold-blooded, thus they were generally stupid. Humans seem to be saying that a life form can only be intelligent if it lives in the "Human Age." And even at that, only humans are "allowed" (according to humans), to have souls, to truly feel joy and pain, to love. Nothing could be further from the truth.

Humans Will Be Cosmic Citizens

Very soon, humanity will enter into *cosmic citizenship* and the old human chauvinist views will have to be left behind. Just wait until humanity meets us! Wait until humanity meets the more "exotic" members of our Space/Dimensional Intelligence! I for one would not want to miss this very special time and I look forward to welcoming humanity into the galaxy with a hearty hug!

You, our precious light workers, will be as pleased as I, and you will help less prepared humans to adjust. You are the teachers, the wise ones. You are the adapters of energy, from human to cosmic frequency. It is you who will help humans gently make the leap.

You will look back and be happily amazed at yourself for living in physical human form but managing to achieve Cosmic Citizenship ahead of time. You are already *here*, my co-worker. You are the bridge between human and alien, between past and future. You are the messenger of the dream and the bringer of the risen frequency!

Because of you, there is Hope, Promise, Potential, and Life.

You will survive these Earth Changes and flourish in a shining new world!

May the healing light of God and goodness surround you, always,

Tibus

This is Meridan.

At least, that is what I am called in Earth terms. I come in goodness and truth. My conceptual name is "He Who Heals." You may think of me as an alien healer.

I suppose my physical appearance would seem quite strange to most Earth people but I have confidence that if you were to meet me, you would judge me for inner worth. You seekers of the light are very good beings.

I am a doctor, both medical and psychic in nature; I am a healer in the universal sense.

I wish to discuss this plague called AIDS which has been unleashed on Earth. Newspapers on Earth have carried articles which say the HIV virus may have been introduced to the human race through experiments to find the cure for malaria by using monkey blood which contained the virus. I am not familiar with Earth's political propaganda, but the medical truth is, this is not the case.

Rather, this information and other similar "possible theories" are an effort on the part of Earth governments to introduce the concept among their people that the HIV virus is human-made, created by human science. They feel they must introduce this concept because it is the truth, and the truth always comes out, eventually.

The governments fear the reaction on the part of the people when it becomes general knowledge that the virus was government made and so they wish to introduce the general concept "softly."

The truth is, the virus was deliberately created and also created with a vaccine. There is also a cure. Both the vaccine and cure are kept from the people.

The powers in charge intended that the victims of HIV be racial minorities, alternative lifestyle people, drug users, and creative types ("Bohemians"). These are the people who are most rebellious and least easy to lead politcally.

World governments do not care if huge numbers of Africans die of the disease because the sufferings of the Third World are a thorn in the side of comfortable civilization.

Several years ago, my co-worker Tibus stated that salt water (a saline solution), was a simple but valuable part of the AIDS cure. There is now documented medical research along this line.

We are asked why we do not channel the cure, but we have! The cure is not desired by those who have power.

We have also channeled the fact that the HIV virus is transmitted in salt water. This is how sea mammals developed a mutated form of immune deficiency illness. The virus was carried through human waste discharges into ocean waters and it mutated from there.

HIV is responsive to salt water; it opens its defenses when in salt water in order to mutate and expand. However, it is vulnerable then, too. This is the time at which is must be attacked.

Our greatest concern is not that every member of the human race will catch it, but rather that the virus, which exists on the DNA (gene) level, will become the norm within the DNA structure. Thus, a jaded evolutionary step will have been taken. Babies will be "normal" when they are born with faulty immune systems and it would then be "normal" for almost all of the human race to die early.

This will not be the case if the human race can take a step upward in spiritual awareness! A jaded genetic step backward such as the immune weakness becoming the norm, will not be taken if the human race can just raise its frequency to the next level.

Humans Must Evolve

The human race must move away from "the end of the race / the end of the world" scenario and go forward into a new reality. This step in itself will leave HIV behind; the human physical vessel will have evolved/grown stronger when the spirit evolves/grows stronger.

Back to the present: We have helped private researchers with concepts and materials necessary to prevent and cure AIDS. We do this through telepathy and inspiration sent to the individual. The preventative vaccine and the cure are not that difficult but researchers who come close to finding them, have disappeared. We may be sealing the fate of a valuable medical person to assist him or her with information. So you can see that we have to think twice when we offer assistance to a researcher.

Few realize that the prevention and the cure for cancer is also known but these would deal a huge financial blow to the very lucrative big business of insurance, hospital care, specialists, chemotherapy, the list is endless. Making big money is preferred to saving lives in the current frequency of reality on Earth.

How can this information help you survive, my friend? Individual humans have the wondrous ability to heal themselves of most cancers. Mother Earth gives miraculous herbs to help also.

AIDS can be beaten, too, by the individual's healing ability but this is much harder to do because it strikes at the DNA level. In a sense, it becomes a part of the individual.

This self-healing ability is not a miracle in our reality, it is simply our way of life. All of our medical efforts are always accompanied by psychic/spiritual healing methods, both from healers (healers/doctors), like myself, and from the ill individual (healing the self).

Of course we never lose sight that healing itself is a miracle and is never accomplished without the presence of the Creator Spirit.

In fact, it is getting in touch with the Creator Spirit on a deep, internal basis, which accomplishes healing. One must *feel and know* that the Creator Spirit lives within one's individual DNA in order to heal the self. One must then *feel and know* that this Creator can change, on a DNA level, what has gone wrong.

The HIV virus might certainly be viewed as The Devil who has infested the DNA. This is an interesting concept for those trying to fight the HIV infection at the cell level through their own psychic imagery. The Creator Spirit is within your DNA, and The Devil has invaded. Through creative visualization, you can perceive the two fighting to the death, and your healthy DNA wins!

I offer this transmission as a helpmate to your survival. Revolutionize how you view disease; also revolutionize how you view the human being.

Medical science does not consider the *whole* being; medical science's view of disease is also too narrow. There is a spiritual/psychic aspect to both the whole being, and to disease.

In closing I reaffirm that all life is sacred and divine.

I will now end transmission.

I AM Meridan.

That is the only message we have ever received from Meridan. But there is another alien healer from whom we hear often. He is Tibus' close friend and has channeled messages to our Star Network since its inception.

Micha is guided by logic and intellect. Yet he and Tibus are very close. This might be surprising, because Tibus is very much spirit-guided. He uses logic but he always opts for "the heart leading the way." This approach bewilders poor extraterrestrial Micha, but the two seem to get along famously.

Micha believes in unconditional love for all life, just as Tibus does. But he believes this is the only logical way to relate to the universe. He finds violence, bigotry, cruelty, greed, and jealousy to be unthinkable behavior. He is an extremely gifted individual in psychic terms, which might surprise someone who thought that "logic" and "psychic" do not go together. In fact, they do, and Micha is living proof of it.

Hello, fellow seekers of enlightenment. I am Micha and I come to you in the light of logic.

A shocking amount of genetic engineering and gene splicing is going on behind the closed doors of governmental/military Earth labs. This research is completely unknown to the common person. Frightening experiments have been attempted, frightening specimens have been created. Humankind must learn to control his cold scientific research which has no universal decency!

Diane, do not be depressed because the outlook is bright as long as you keep your eyes fixed on the highest star.

I wish to discuss The Virus for a moment: Allow me to assure you that viruses are a form of life which can be fought effectively through psychic/spiritual energy. More than any other form of life, viruses respond to this!

For the most part, viruses belong to a particular level of existence. The current frequency on Earth is ripe for The Virus to flourish; like nuclear energy, these are something which exist at a particular point in a planet's evolution. Viruses cannot exist when the frequency is a higher one.

When you stop to think of it, viruses came into Earth's reality about the time nuclear energy did. Oh, you might say cancer was known in the past but called something else. Yes, some viruses and cancers did exist in the past under different names, but the truth is, viruses have mushroomed in kind and number in the last 50 years. This is their day, so to speak. And this (the current reality), is their world!

As Meridan has stressed, a high vibration is not a fertile ground for a virus. They cannot exist in a world which has a high frequency of thinking, feeling, and being.

The Virus will be left behind when the survivors of the present reality, move onward.

I leave you for now with the thought that "survival of the fittest" does not apply to the physical world alone, it also applies to the spiritual world! There is the key to survival, my friend!

In unconditional love, I AM Micha

Tibus has sent us a transmission related to Micha's message which we feel will be helpful to you in these Change Times:

This is Tibus. I come to you in love and light.

The HIV virus is a real threat to not only the human species but to other higher mammals, such as sea mammals. This virus mutates and affects many other species also, or will soon. And viruses do have a nasty habit of mutating!

But remember always that *the virus is influenced relatively easily by psychic energy.*

We do not see this disease wiping out the human species. But, let us think again of our continuum: At "1" is the HIV virus already having peaked. It becomes extinct in the near future, the human race having developed an immunity and/or found a vaccine.

At "10" on the continuum, the human race is utterly wiped out by AIDS.

You can see now how this continuum relates to the Reality Continuum we have discussed. Just as a Doomsday "10" need not happen, neither should this "worst case HIV scenario" occur. *You have the ability to create the future!*

A "10" will not happen if people do not pour energy into the negative scenario of "the complete decimation of the human race and the complete destruction of the planet!"

You must realize that you can create a very negative future as well as a very positive one!

Achieving Psychic Integrity

This brings us to the concept of "psychic integrity."

A person should not become involved in "things psychic" unless he or she is truly able to adhere to *trying to create the most positive of possible outcomes.*

Some people give lip service to this concept, but when the latest "scare scenario" comes down the road which appeals to some aspect of their psychology, they jump on the band wagon.

"The Big One is coming for real this year, on this or that date!"

Or, "Alien reptoids who eat humans are landing for lunch!"

Or, "Everyone who thinks they are channeling higher beings is really channeling mean little grey aliens!"

Or, "AIDS is going to wipe us all out in ten years!"

The list is endless. Diane has been involved in the psychic world and the New Age for fourteen years, and she has heard every rumor. Sadly, she has heard more negative psychic "excitement" than positive psychic "excitement" from well meaning New Agers.

Rumors always abound. Fingers are pointed. Fads come and go.

Few realize that they retard the raising of the frequency when they go off on these illogical tangents. But they are!

It hurts the future itself when all these dead end roads are taken. Why wait for the Big One, really believing it will happen this time? Aren't you adding creative energy to this event when you embrace the concept of it happening?

This is basic metaphysics and also, basic quantum physics. To be a seeker of the light and a student of the psychic world, you must realize this truth once and for all!

Do Not Add Psychic Fuel to Negative Realities

Do not add psychic fuel to the negative fire. Instead, keep your eyes on the highest star and be positive.

A slightly different problem when dealing with psychic energy is what we call "*the fear factor*". Human beings have a lot of fear hidden within their souls, especially when they deal with "things psychic" which have been considered as "evil" by organized religions for centuries. Humans know better than this, but that subconscious *fear factor* remains.

Is the unknown always evil? This is a question the human soul still wonders. (The answer is, "No!").

However, there are negative energies out there in the universe. And when fear rises in the human soul, these negative energies and entities see an open door, and rush in. They feed off blind fear.

And when humans deal with the psychic world, there is often blind fear.

So, a psychic experience can turn negative simply because of the fear factor. It is a self-perpetuating and self-defeating emotionally charged energy within the human species.

The *fear factor* is very dangerous because once fear is created, it gives energy to the most negative point on the continuum. I repeat: *Fear is the greatest enemy when one is dealing with "things psychic."*

New Agers sincerely embrace the concepts of love and light, but some do not practice *psychic integrity.* They tend to rush from one paranoid scenario to another, spending much money to support the scenario (books, tapes, etc.). They also do not hesitate to become frightened, they do not practice psychic control. It is the responsibility of every individual who enters the psychic world to control the fear factor. This literally makes the difference between a beautiful experience and a terrible one.

We must keep our eyes on the highest star. The problems I have described are two of the largest obstacles to the human race being able to raise the frequency.

If we do keep our eyes on the highest star, we cannot lose. A new day will dawn!

May the healing light of God and goodness surround you, always,
Tibus

Veritan chimes in: The regular readers of my **Change Times Quarterly** publication, will recognize Veritan, the sometimes befuddled alien who is just learning to send his thoughts telepathically to a human. We've been asked to include his contribution to the subjects of noninterference in Earth history, AIDS, and cancer.

This is Veritan. I come to you in the light of intelligence.

Once our existence is accepted by virtually all humans (once our existence becomes a part of the mass human consciousness), we will be able to "interfere" more, in order to save situations and individuals (for instance, those suffering from AIDS or cancer).

This is not to say we can go around saving all dangerous situations and all life forms who are dying. Our powers of precognition would make it possible to avert nearly all death on the planet. But this would be a travesty against nature herself.

Is it not the nature of all life to live and die, then to live again? It is a cycle, a gift the Creator Spirit gave to all.

We cannot and should not keep everything and everyone alive "forever." This would be a state of complete stagnation, against the universal law of Change/Momentum.

It is our belief that the only true death is indeed stagnation of the spirit.

Sometimes I wonder how some humans perceive the bright New Age because they seem to feel it will be a time of no change, no life/death cycle, no growth, only a "love and light" status quo.

The way of The Creator must be wisely perceived and taken to the heart and soul; one cannot design a stagnant new world in one's own image (that is, one's perception of a never-changing happy world).

The Creator gives life, destroys it, then gives this same cosmic spark, new life again. And so the cycle goes.

UFO Encounters Are Coming

In reference to knowledge of our existence becoming a part of the mass human consciousness, I confirm that we are increasing our contact with humans the world over, thus *many* UFO sightings and encounters with UFO occupants are coming in the final years of the 20th Century.

Now that the Change Times has descended full force on the planet, it is up to us to make our existence and presence known to human beings, in no uncertain terms. In this way, we make it possible for our help to manifest more and more. There will be many "interferences" and "miracles" on Earth in the future.

Once we do exist in the reality of every human's consciousness, then the noninterference directive is not dominant in our policy toward Earth. Once a race enters cosmic citizenship, the noninterference directive no longer applies for the most part, because you will have joined our galactic community. You will be us just as Tibus is human and is one of us.

I thank you for listening to my thoughts. I am honored to be working toward helping to save your planet. It is a beautiful planet indeed! I remind you that "it" is really a "she." Your planet has a magnificent female persona. Her spiritual presence, whom we call Gaia, is among the most lyrical and mesmerizing in the galaxy. (Yes, all planets who support life do have a spiritual presence). I know that we will talk again, my co-worker.

I send you logic, tempered with love and compassion,

Veritan

A second transmission from Veritan on this urgent subject gives us further helpful information and insight:

Hello, my friends. This is Veritan once again, having gotten the hang to channeling to some degree. I come to you in the light of logic.

I wish to give you an update on the dreaded Ebola virus and in a more general way, a new report on the many mutant viruses and other organisms, which are springing to life, entering into your Reality Base, due primarily to Earth's failing immune system.

I use the word "failing" but I do not aim to imply that it is a downward spiral which cannot be stopped. It can be rectified slowly, over time, through drastic scientific and especially spiritual measures.

Dormant Organisms Awaken

Organisms which have been dormant for millennia are coming to life because of the weakened planetary immune system; these organisms essentially did not exist because the planet was strong enough to render them inactive. Now, she cannot keep them from becoming animated.

Also, organisms from outer space are entering Earth's atmosphere and finding no strong planetary immune system to keep them from beginning on Earth. The ozone layer, when it was healthy and complete, stopped such organisms cold in their tracks. But we all know the ozone layer is in serious trouble.

All is connected, my friends. All in linked. Balance is indeed a sacred commodity. Because when a planetary immune system fails, so do immune systems of individual life forms such as sea mammals, human beings, and a tragic host of other animals and plants. All is connected. All is linked. When the planet fails, the human being fails. When oh when will humankind learn this?

Regarding Ebola specifically: There have been many rumors of an Ebola epidemic in the United States in the final four years of the century. "Is this true?" we are asked.

The answer is: Yes, in one branch of reality, Ebola sweeps through the population of the United States killing three fifths of its population. Yet, in another branch reality, not one case of Ebola is reported.

In between are an infinite number of branch realities. As an example, in one of the alternate realities, 10,006 people die of Ebola in the U.S. in one year. In another alternate reality, 10,007 people die of Ebola. In the first alternate reality, one person was saved through an extra effort of healing prayer and an extra amount of loving medical care.

The Danger of Absolute Predictions

The danger of absolute predictions such as, "Huge Ebola outbreak in the U.S.," is that it tends to cement one reality. The power of the mass consciousness *expects* this reality and thus the chances of it happening are increased many fold.

I also want to add that I do not aim to stress that Ebola breaking out in the United States is any bigger tragedy than Ebola breaking out anywhere else in the world. Life is sacred anywhere and just because human beings live in the Third World does not make their lives any less valuable.

Back to branch realities: What must be realized once and for all is that *the future is wide open. It is not written in stone. It can be changed!*

The power of each individual's mind and soul is tremendous indeed. The power of many minds/souls is enormous. The branch reality wherein there are no reported Ebola cases in the United States is as valid as the other extreme, or any of the points along the continuum.

You can make it not happen! It need not happen. There is no future written in stone.

We hope to work with psychics and channels as well as with scientists so that when they make predictions such as this, they present them in such a way as to remind people that the future is wide open and that they can make a difference in seeing that a prediction does not happen. Remember that predictions and prophecies are there to help us make a better future. If they predict a terrible event, we can then work to stop this event from taking place. We can work both spiritually and actively to stop it, thus create an alternate reality where it did not happen.

Remember that viruses are especially influenced by psychic energies. If you work against these viruses, you build your own immunities. Wish them out of existence, my friends! Perhaps this is simplistic, but I promise you that they do respond to psychic energies.

On the Home Side we have known for a long time that one of the major threats to life itself during Earth's Change Times is the rapid mutation and "waking up" of existing viruses and similar organisms and the introduction into the ecosystem of other organisms from outer space. This phenomenon has occurred time and time again on other planets as first this world, then that world, faced its particular Change Times before its evolutionary step upward to cosmic citizenship.

Atmosphere Damaged

Almost always, the world's atmosphere is damaged, thus allowing organisms to "wake up" or to enter the atmosphere. But we also know that psychic energy is specifically and dynamically very effective in influencing such organisms. We know for starters that such organisms respond to psychic energy when they wake up or arrive. *They sense when a world is in trouble.*

There are many similar cases in nature: When an immune system is weakened by the HIV virus, a secondary infection sets in, saying, "This is my time to strike!" This "sensing" is a primitive form of the psychic 6th sense in these organisms. It is subject to psychic impression, whether sensing the original weakness or sensing a more advanced psychic source who says, "Go away and dry up!" *This more advanced force is you!*

We know that there are scientific explanations as to why negative organisms victimize a weakened immune system, but we have told you that The Scientific and The Spiritual meet on up the road! For organisms to invade the ecosystem of a weakened planetary force, this is both a scientific and a spiritual phenomenon. They do not contradict, they are the same phenomenon put in different terms. Both are valid.

So as to the accuracy of an Ebola or other "mutant virus" epidemic sweeping the United States, I can only repeat that the door to the future is wide open. The combined psychic force of life forms on the planet, as well as the planetary life force herself, create the future. A huge "plus" on the side of a positive outcome is always that *all life really wants to live, really wants (therefore), a positive outcome.*

If you do not believe this, look how many life forms survive against all odds in times of extreme hardship. All too often, we look at how many die (the half empty glass), but I can assure you beyond a shadow of a doubt, that the combined life force of every lifeform, plus the planet herself, is on your side as you work and struggle to make a positive, less tragic Change Times.

In the light of logic,
I AM Veritan

As we complete our subchapter on **The Viral Threat,** we will let Micha, the healer, have the last word.

My friends, this is Micha.

The HIV crisis in itself threatens the continuation of the entire human race, because it has long since moved out of the "high risk" groups and into the mainstream of the populace. In 50 years, how far will the virus have progressed?

Remember, it has the ability to mutate rapidly and has in fact done this since it first got introduced. We acknowledge that government experiments originated this virus which mimics the human immune system, thus tricking the usual human defenses against infection into nonaction. Genetic experiments not only originated the virus but were responsible for introducing it into "non-mainstream" groups such as homosexuals and intravenous drug users.

Karmic Cesspool Created

Because of their horrendous deed of creating this virus, and then introducing it into the human gene pool, these individuals in government have created a karmic cesspool for themselves which is more dreadful than the disease they created. We stress that the innocent victims of this immune affliction in no way "deserve" the disease any more than you or I do.

The key to any of the human race surviving the HIV threat is this: Other events will create a Change Point which will raise the frequency, literally creating a new dimension. The higher vibration which will belong to humanity in this new dimension will fight off the HIV virus in a way which the human spirit cannot do in the present reality. The virus thrives in the present reality but will not be native to, or belong in, the new dimension.

Thus there is not fifty years left at the current frequency of existence; indeed, there are not twenty years left! The killer virus will not have a chance to reach full potential.

However, I stress that despite the fact that the change in dimension will nullify the HIV threat, research on finding a preventative measure and a cure, must continue! Research on finding drugs which retard the virus once it is in the human body, must continue also.

Allow me to explain *why:* First I would like to draw an analogy to the fact that one should not sit back and wait for Judgement Day, figuring any effort is useless meanwhile. If there is a Judgement Day, what would you like to be judged on? Certainly on the efforts you made (or didn't make), while waiting for Judgement Day!

We on the Home Side do not champion the concept of "Judgement Day" but we do believe a Change Point is coming up. The world must be of as high a frequency as humanly possible at this point. Lives can be saved from the HIV threat before this Change Point.

If you do not try on "this side" of the Change Point, that Change Point will not occur! A catch-22, as humans say!

If you do not try on "this side," you are sealing the fate of the planet, then Doomsday is at hand.

Making the Change Point Happen

The Change Point must be forced to occur. Like any change, like any momentum, there must be *energy* behind it. Pushing!

Change does not happen without *energy* being applied; this is scientific law. That energy is coming from, and will come from, *you*, my friend.

It comes from you as you work to make a better world, as you work to save a world!

Incidentally, it is true that the prevention method and cure for AIDS is already known. But these will not be released by certain individuals within government structures. So, we must consider that they do not exist. The prevention and cure of the affliction must be discovered "again" by enlightened researchers.

Again, we remind you that a high spiritual vibration is an excellent defense against your own immune system being attacked.

This is precious knowledge for you to know in order to survive!

You are familiar with the super strain of tuberculosis which is manifesting particularly in poor economic areas and which is connected to the HIV virus in many cases. The human body seems incapable of fighting this new TB germ and antibiotics are ineffective.

There is also a "flesh eating bug" which is a mutated, new form of life created in genetic laboratories. This "bug" ingests human flesh extremely rapidly, like a speeded-up gangrene infection. It causes death almost overnight.

And we cannot forget the horrendous Ebola, a viral disease which makes AIDS look downright benign.

I have mentioned these four because I wish to point out that these lifeforms display a kind of intelligence. Of course, describing how any germ works makes it sound as though it has intelligence, when in fact the microbiological world works on a different dynamic. However, these new viruses, and bacteria coupled with viruses, do have an evil kind of intelligence ("evil" because they have no soul, no conscience).

Great Evil Created

This was given to them when created in gene splicing experiments in laboratories. "Intelligence" has never before applied in the microbiotic world. The evil that has been created is great indeed.

But because there is intelligence, these viruses and bacteria can be fought very successfully on a psychic level!

Most of all, these new super bugs can be prevented from striking through actively maintaining a high spiritual frequency.

As you meditate to save Earth, you may also be saving yourself from one of the new diseases.

Your communion with nature can also work this miracle for you. Being very close to nature is a real deterrent against catching one of these unnatural bugs. Mother Nature did not create these life forms and so they do not have natural balance.

We also recommend that you take plenty of the natural antibiotic, garlic. It is truly a miraculous herb. The Dracula legend about garlic stopping evil was not so far off. Also, the natural solution of lemon and honey is a miraculous helpmate to help you survive this Day of the Super Bug.

On the Home Side, we call any change you affect in your body, biokinesis. You know that telekinesis is the moving of objects with your mind. Pirokinesis is the starting of fires with your mind's power. Biokinesis is affecting a change within your body, with your mind.

Psychic powers affect the submolecular world!

Consciousness (intelligence), travels on submolecular waves and particles. Therefore, the "intelligence" given these super bugs, can be fought psychically.

In the light of logic,

I AM Micha

And so, our alien friends have given us a blueprint for surviving The Virus, which is, tragically, a huge threat in these days of Earth Change.

Obviously, healthy living and maintaining the physical body in top form are recommended also. And make every effort not to make yourself vulnerable or exposed to HIV or any of the new, genetically engineered plagues of modern humanity.

The Threat From Mother Nature

The threat of natural cataclysmic disaster stems from two sources: One is what humankind has caused to happen. This includes the depleted ozone layer, global warming, rain forest destruction, pollution and nuclear or chemical contamination of land and sea. Sadly, the list is growing.

The threat of natural cataclysmic disaster also comes from volcanic eruptions, earthquakes, and tidal waves. This second source of potential global destruction is seemingly not related to the damage humankind has caused.

Of course, there are areas which overlap. The climate change caused by global warming causes some areas to experience drought while other areas get too much rain. The balance has been interrupted. Because of drought, there are many more wild fires, in brush and forest. While a forest fire caused by lightning would seem to be an "act of God," we must remember, that if the land were not so parched, the lightning might not have started such an inferno.

In a similar way, the winds from a hurricane might seem natural, not caused by humanity. But huge tropical storms are forming with much more frequency and severity because the climate is changing. Global warming again plays a part. So it is difficult to perceive just how far humankind's damage to the environment stretches.

Nature is Angry

What we have been told in channelings is that Mother Nature is angry. If you perceive the planet as a living entity, then you must allow that she has emotions as well as physical attributes. These emotions may be alien to us, because a planetary entity is quite different from an individual human entity. Yet, she is our mother.

Just as God made us in His image, so the Mother Planet made us in Her image. In fact, are we not saying exactly the same thing here? God/Goddess made us in His/Her image!

In your special place in nature, you can feel her emotions.

On a beautiful spring morning, you can feel the joy she feels at the renewal of life. On a moody autumn evening, you can feel her melancholy, contemplating winter and the death of the formerly young spring leaves and plants.

In channeling after channeling, we have been told that now Gaia, the spirit of the planet, is angry. She is hurt. Her most accomplished creation, humanity, has damaged her almost beyond repair. Let me share with you now some of these channelings not simply to show you her anger, but because they do give hope! These channelings give answers as to what has to be done, and on how to survive.

Diane, this is Veritan. I come to you in the light of logic.

I have visited many worlds in this galaxy and most of them are dead worlds with no lifeform capable of living on them. A few of these have lifeforms within them (subsurface).

Of course, "most of them" is a relative concept, because when you have billions of worlds in the galaxy, then a mere two million worlds which support life, is still a very small percentage.

The worlds which support life are not infinite in number but are a precious few indeed. We all must treasure a world such as Earth who supports life so beautifully.

I notice humans tend to throw around the term "infinite" without stopping to truly comprehend its meaning. Can one have 17 galaxies with an infinite number of stars in them? No, because if the first galaxy is truly infinite, it will encompass all the other galaxies. In a sense, this is a definition of the entire universe: an infinite galaxy. I wish to speak specifically now of this galaxy, the one you humans call The Milky Way.

Life In The Milky Way

Within The Milky Way, life on a planet which circles a star, is a relatively rare occurrence. There is (for lack of a better word), other-dimensional life on some of them, but not 3-dimensional, physical life which lives on the surface. On a few, there are life forms which "swim" through the atmosphere but which cannot live on the surface. Of course there are combinations of these which "swim" but which rest on the surface also, similar to Earth's amphibians. There are a great number of variations.

And yet, with all the combinations possible, I repeat my original statement: Life in any form which circles a star in The Milky Way is a relatively rare occurrence.

My object in the above paragraph is twofold: To express how many planets there are in the galaxy, because even though life is rare, there are millions of planets which do sustain some form of life!

Secondly, I wish to remind you how precious life is, in any form. How rare, how precious. Even in the form of an ant. Or a robin. Or a daisy. Or algae.

If Earth had 5 percent more oxygen, all would be in a state of consumption by burning (oxidizing). Life could not live as you know it. If Earth had 5% less oxygen, it would not sustain life as you know it. Let us cherish the delicate balance!

As an example of life on nearby planets: In the Solar System, Venus, Mars, Jupiter, Saturn and Uranus have other-dimensional (non-corporeal) life forms. Mercury and Pluto have no life in any form. There are a few smaller planets of which your scientists are only now becoming aware. Several of these as well as the satellites of several major planets, do have life, but not as you know it.

When someone claims he is from Venus, or has met someone from Venus, they are talking about a life-essence which is Venusian, not Terran (Earth). But the physical body is human, not Venusian, since there is no such thing as a Venusian corporeal body.

Of the planets listed above, Venus' other-dimensional life forms are most advanced, although they are not as high on the awareness ladder as many races originating outside the Solar System. Venusians do not, as a group, participate in helping us (and you), help Earth. They mean well and are good souls but, if humankind is an adolescent race, so are Venusians. Life is relatively new on Venus. This is as-should-be, because Earth and Venus are sibling planets of Sol, their Mother Sun.

Mars, on the other hand, sustained a formidable civilization at one time. Mars is the older brother of Earth and Venus. But he did not survive his Change Times. The worst case "10" became reality on his Reality Continuum. Doomsday.

Many lessons were learned by those of us who had clustered around Mars, attempting to help him through the crisis which befalls every planet which has intelligent life.

Yes, Mars' soul energy is male. Venus and Earth are female.

At any rate, many lessons were learned from Mars; one is that direct interference, though well intentioned, never works. This applies especially to the intelligent races of the planets which circle Sol. The native race must experience the lessons to be learned, they must go through the hardships and the difficult steps.

Hard Lessons Cannot Be Ignored

If they are spared those hard lessons, they do not learn them; Doomsday is only prolonged a bit longer. The agony is prolonged. But the end still comes.

Who or what lives on Mars now? Only the echoes of past life forms. Ghosts? Yes, but these "entity echoes" are a form of life whereas most Earth ghosts are not life forms but merely "replays" in the groove of reality.

We of Space/Dimensional Intelligence have bases on Mars because it is very close to Earth, yet it is safe for us; Earth militaries can cause us great danger. We know these "Martian entity echoes" (ghosts), well because they are difficult to live with. They can be very capricious and mischievous, almost like a poltergeist.

Jupiter, Saturn, and Uranus have life forms who are very "remote." That is, they are not highly conscious in any way we can discover. They seem to be a part of the basic soul of their planet. It is difficult to discern them from simply "the spirit of Uranus" for example. But they do have individual components of consciousness.

Incidentally, when I say I have visited worlds, I do not mean I have stood on the surface of Uranus. There is no solid surface on which to stand. We define "visit" as having placed our craft in orbit around the planet so that we can then examine it closely through instruments and by flying closer in scout craft if possible.

You cannot do even this with some planets. We have discovered that the spirit of some worlds is hostile and wild, so it would be rather like entering a dark forest which contains many rattlesnakes. The snake itself, while intelligent, is a wild creature and strikes out almost mindlessly. Planets can be this way, too.

Science would tell you that you simply cannot fly close to Jupiter's surface because storms would swallow up the craft while it was still above Jupiter. But spiritually we would say that the essence which is Jupiter (just as Gaia is the Earth's essence), is wild and nearly mindless. Science and spirituality do not contradict each other, they are complimentary as this example illustrates. This is one lesson the human race is about to learn!

Again, I remind you how precious Gaia is! She is not only highly intelligent, but she is wise and basically loving. She has created some wild creatures, but she herself is a beautiful, nurturing soul.

Gaia's lifeforms care about their own; just think how ape mothers love their young. Even alligator mothers make an effort to protect the young. Gaia instills care and love in her children.

Life On Earth Is Precious

Gaia herself is a rare combination of circumstances which make life extremely dynamic on Terra. Gaia is a rare and beautiful lady. That may not be a logical statement, it is a bit (I admit) – poetic. But she is poetry and there is no other way to express it.

I will end my solar travel log for now. I know anyone reading this is curious about other worlds; I also know that in your soul, you remember other worlds, even if your conscious mind does not. It is a wondrous thing to travel to other worlds, it is something the soul does not forget. I am indeed fortunate to be a star traveler. Someday, you will have that good fortune again also. The stars await.

I AM Veritan

This is Tibus. I come to you in love and light.

My teachings stress humankind's connection to Mother Earth. Enlightened people in particular must form a personal, working relationship to Gaia, who is the Earth's living spirit. This is the cornerstone to surviving into the new, higher dimension.

For the enlightened person, it is not enough to simply love nature. This relationship with Gaia must be consciously formed; you must learn to communicate with Gaia in most specific ways, and be able to at the drop of a hat.

In return, you will find Gaia communicating with you in ways you never dreamed possible. Even though you may have been close to nature all your life, it is not the same as actively forming a conscious link with Gaia. Events will happen which take your breath away in wonder and inspiration; Gaia is an amazing lifeform! After all, she is the planetary life force and just look at how wondrous this magnificent force is, all across the planet.

Learn To Understand Gaia's Communication

You will find Gaia communicating with you in terms of symbolism and synchronicities. The Native Americans, the ancient Celts, the Australian Aborigines, and other tribes close to nature, were/are able to perceive the living symbolism of the Mother Planet.

This is not a distant, cold symbolism such as, "You might decide an eagle symbolizes the soul of one who has died." Instead, these tribes perceive a dynamic, living, changing symbolism integrated into reality itself: "The eagle transforms into the one who has died, and he flies through the air to new life, dropping a feather at a significant moment." The symbolism *is*. It is truth as much as any other aspect of reality. It is real.

Modern humanity has the wrong definition of symbolism. It is considered distant, detached, hard to understand. But it is a living phenomenon which mingles with daily reality. The soul of a person who has passed on does enter the eagle. It is a reality. A truth. He says good-bye in a conscious way to his loved ones before he flies onward to New Life. The physical eagle can return to his life, to be a bird again, after the symbolic reality is done.

In the same way, Gaia gives us synchronicities as meaningful, helpful communications in our lives. We of the higher realms cherish this gift from Mother Earth beyond expression. There is indeed no such thing as coincidence.

When working in the natural realm, astounding "coincidences" will begin to happen for you as you break through to conscious communication and oneness with Gaia. Is it a coincidence that you found a rose in your yard this morning when just last night you were thinking how your mother loved roses? The loving energy which was/is your mother, has worked with Gaia to give you an inspiring synchronicity! You have been given a priceless message from both the soul who is your mother and from Gaia. This is a small example of the sheer excitement and inspiration one finds when being a conscious lover and friend to Gaia.

The miraculous truth is, you are helping the living entity Earth survive the current traumatic times when nature is taking such a beating from humanity. One enlightened individual can make a huge difference!

Earth has been polluted, contaminated, decimated, raped, and ignored. Your conscious love will give her strength to regenerate and to flourish again. She asks only to be recognized and loved by her human children; she wants only to have a reflection again in the mirror of reality. (Her animal children do recognize and love her, and it is they who have kept her alive).

Love Is A Two-Way Street

I stress that the two way street between humankind and the Planetary Mother is a miracle in itself. When Gaia helps you heal, she helps to heal herself. And when you heal Gaia, you also heal yourself.

When you help Gaia survive, you help your own survival. When she helps you survive, she helps her own life force!

The Creator Spirit (God) is embodied on Earth as Gaia. It seems absurd to worship a God who sits in heaven somewhere while destroying God-on-Earth (the planet). The life force and spirit of nature is God! Why does humanity focus on a nebulous humanoid, male God when God is all around, right on the planet? He/She is the planet!

Yes, other planets have life forces, so I am not saying that God is restricted to Earth. The cosmos is timeless and infinite; many worlds develop a persona. The God Force is endless, throughout the universe.

The mass which is a planet often develops an entity presence, whether it supports life, or not. A planet which does not support life of some kind, then continues along the awareness ladder and develops a conscious soul. This soul infuses life into life forms; it is a miraculous catch 22 that a planet who develops consciousness infuses life into specific life forms, but also, those life forms give momentum to the planet's living soul.

I also stress it is your responsibility to know the more familiar forms of life which Gaia has to offer, and help them.

I speak of "stray" dogs and cats and other animals in need. Also look into the nature of the plants which are all around you and which you tend to not appreciate.

Be active in environmental causes! This helps your own survival too.

These are your responsibilities as an enlightened cosmic citizen. Happily, this gives you great joy; giving brings happiness. So this responsibility is not a heavy or drudging one.

Enlightened individuals actually crave contact with nature and become very depressed when they cannot get to this wondrous energy. Nature has been an adventure for you since you were a child. She is your confidante, friend, your joy, and even your lover.

As an enlightened individual, you are empathetic to others. Your extreme sensitivity is actually an extra dose of Mother Nature within you. This is the

God Spark, enhanced. What better survival tool?

Do What Is Right For You

I, Tibus, teach that enlightened individuals must join together spiritually from time to time, especially in order to heal Gaia. Our **Star Network** pre-sets Cleansing/Healing Days in which we all participate psychically. Throughout the years, I have given numerous meditations, often using natural objects to assist meditation and prayer. These range from crystals and gemstones to feathers, leaves and nuts. I have never taught that objects are essential to successful meditation and contact; if they help you focus and if you can blend your energies with them, then use them. If you feel better without using objects, then that is fine, too.

In the same way, I have always taught that formal, ritualized meditation is right if that is what works for you, but if you do better with informal walks in nature or simply sitting still and clearing your mind, then rituals are not necessary. It is good to alternate ritualized meditation and prayer with a more casual energy, such as a refreshing walk in nature in which you simply see what Gaia has to say to you.

At the close of this book, we will give you several meditations which *work.*

In general, I feel the human race needs to unstructure its spiritual and religious beliefs, so I do not stress that a specific structure or words need be used.

If the orthodox Christian religion could unstructure itself, not having the many intricate rituals, doctrines and dogmas which each smaller division of Christianity insists on, and the Moslem religion could un-structure itself, the two huge Earth religions would find they both believe intensely in one God whatever His name, that both teach good behavior, and so forth. It is the petty rules and regulations which convince the less enlightened of both religions that they are vastly superior to the followers of the other religion. Thus the human race is divided and hates itself.

Our teachings do not pretend to constitute a religion and we are quite happy about this. We do offer a blueprint for enlightened souls who seek to survive and flourish in a new dimension, one in which natural Earth still exists. When you stop to consider it, no one can survive if the planet does not, so this is the obvious priority!

I will close transmission for this time, sending you my unconditional love.

May the healing light of God and goodness surround you, always,

Tibus

Veritan and Tibus, as members of our Space/Dimensional Intelligence friends, have shared their knowledge about the state of our Mother Planet in the two preceding channelings. Now I would like to share with you a transmission which I received during a howling wind storm in Ireland, which is directly from a nature spirit. Nature spirits *are* the Mother Planet, expressing herself through a specialized aspect. As such, nature spirits can be of tremendous help in facilitating contact between we humans and the planet herself.

This is Elea. I am the Spirit of the Wind!

You have not heard from me before, Diane, but I am a being who intends no harm. Outside your cottage, there are Gale Force 10 winds blowing. You have watched the evergreen tree outside your window bending nearly in half, and when you stepped outside for a few moments, your breath was taken away by the wild, strong gusts of wind. This free spirit howls across the fields in the back of your cottage and through the forest nearby, sounding like a freight train as it rushes through limbs and branches of the big old trees.

This wild wind is me, Elea! I have had many names given to me throughout the ages, and I answer to any of them, and to none of them.

The wind outside is a celebration. I am celebrating! I am celebrating New Life, I am celebrating Springtime. Yes, the force of my being may make it difficult for some new, young creatures; wee lambs huddle against their mothers, and baby birds cling to their nests. However, this adversity will make them strong and able to endure later on.

My intent is not evil. I know I do damage sometimes, when anger within Mother Nature expresses itself through my power. But I myself am not an evil being.

The gentle breeze turns sailboats toward a safe harbor and moves the arms of windmills for energy. Humankind must learn to harness my power more for this energy usage. To use me for energy is something humankind has known for millennia but to use me seems much too easy, too simple, and he does not bother to use me much these days. No, humankind wants something "higher tech." Something which will make more money for the already wealthy few. This is a tragedy because he contaminates his planet with nuclear and other harmful energies, while I remain ignored.

The Perfect Energy Source

I am free, and boundless in abundance, a perfect energy source. I am pleased that the wind as an alternate energy source is being experimented with in a few areas of the world.

When you stepped out into my rising and ebbing currents a few moments ago, Diane, I hooked a ride with you, back into the cottage. That is, my conscious spirit did, because I now have a message for you and your friends.

In the last year, I realize I have done much damage in the form of many large hurricanes, unexpected "freak" tornadoes, terrible winter blizzards, and uncommonly bad typhoons. My mother is Mother Nature. When she beckons me, and she demands that I do something which reflects her own despair and anger, I must comply.

Putting this same thought in a human way, because humankind has caused gaping holes in the ozone, burned rain forests, and so on, there is a global warming going on, causing the waters of the world to rise. These create strange currents and wind streams which snowball into vicious storms. When summoned by these currents and streams, my power builds and becomes mighty.

Then death and destruction follow.

Mother Nature, who is mother to us all, does not usually remain angry long, and the storm abates. But her hurt, anger, and despair go on these days, because the fairest of her children, humankind, has nearly destroyed her. The destruction I am doing during the Change Times is only a reflection, a cause and effect phenomenon, of the real destruction done by humans!

Diane, I am giving you this insight, sharing myself with you this "gale force" afternoon, because you and enlightened humans everywhere are welcome to communicate with me; in fact, I beg you to do so in the days to come! To summon the Spirit of the Wind is not a difficult feat.

I urge you to do this, because when you work with me as the shaman would, you actually lessen my power during these angry days. You can alleviate and heal Mother Nature's anger and hurt through your healing meditative communications with her directly, too. The two of us are always hand in hand.

To my enlightened human friends: You may be humble and think that your psychic power is not great enough to offset the power of the wind. This is simply not true. Modern humanity thinks it sounds too silly to "talk to the wind" but that is their ignorance and lack of understanding. Not yours, not mine.

Humans of ancient times communicated with me. I cannot always be calmed completely, but my destructive power can always be lessened through psychic communication.

Wind damage is not the main destructive force of the Change Times, but my power figures prominently in much of the forthcoming destruction, as evidenced by the many storms of the past year. It hurts me in particular to hurt and kill animals in the wild and other innocent lifeforms. I am asking you all to work with me so that the harm I do can be held to a minimum. I stress that I am a servant of another's spiritual powers. Mother Nature is that spiritual power whom I ultimately answer to, but I can be calmed by your spiritual power. I respond to good energies, I do not want to be angry and destructive.

Water Is Miraculous

Diane, you have worked with your clients and readers on the psychic power of Water. Like Wind, Water has a conscious spirit with whom you can communicate. Water reflects the molecular fabric of the universe itself. When you meditate by a still pond, it is as if you are looking at the fabric of reality.

Through positive creative visualization, you can envision a more positive reality as you gaze at the still water. This can literally influence the reality of the world. Still water was the forerunner of the crystal ball, and ancient people used still water often for psychic visualization, in order to influence the future.

In the same way, the flame of a candle representing the element of Fire can be used.

Finally, Earth herself is a powerful psychic commodity.

These are the Four Basic Elements (we will look into these again later in the book). Know us well. Know my companions, Water, Fire, and Earth. Know me, The Air you breathe! Work with us, we beg of you, because we *all*need this planet! It is our home. She must be saved!

I am Elea, closing transmission.

Now, from a nature spirit who is what humans call "a wood sprite" comes a message of tolerance and wisdom. "Naomi" came to me in Ireland also, when I lived near the Castle Morris Forest in County Kilkenny. Here is her message.

I am called Naomi, and the forest you now walk through, is my home. I have been here for thousands of years and I am blessed in that my forest was not cut when so many of the Irish forests were chopped down to make the English ships of war.

Something which is very important in these critical days is to consider Earth spirits and entities with the same fairness as you consider space spirits and entities. Do not assume that we nature spirits are automatically inferior because our home source is Earth. We have much of value to say also to you. Many of us are quite enlightened. We can teach. And we know that you have much to give to us. We welcome the open doors of communication which good humans have created!

This prejudice toward "Earth energies" is one of which Tibus has often spoken. Yet, we know that it is difficult to get rid of old teachings and bias. This bias started when organized religions attempted to discredit "nature worship" by stating that all the entities within that worship system were "demonic" or at least, inferior to human beings, and of course, inferior to those deities worshipped by the orthodox religions.

This is sad, because we do not hold *any* being as inferior or demonic. At any rate, as Spiritualism attempted to revive the "Old Ways" and yet be considered a church within respectable boundaries, it introduced the concept of "elementals." Within this family were "cute little beings" such as leprechauns, elves, fairies, sprites, and gnomes.

Nature Spirits As Humanoids

It is quite true that sometimes we manifest from our dimension(s) into your dimension, as small humanoids. It is true that we often use humor and display what seems to humans to be nonsensical behavior. But it is time that humankind understand the nature of interaction between dimensions, and stop assuming we are "cute but not as evolved as humans," or "like little children who do silly things."

Certainly there are those among us who might fit this description (although the description in itself is condescending), but the vast majority of us are wise and ancient beings of the light.

It is very difficult to coordinate actions perfectly between dimensions, so that reality is identical in both. When we come into your dimension, this problem is why our actions seem out of synch.

To describe most of us would be very similar to describing a star guardian (higher being), from space. And in fact, the guardians of some enlightened humans are from other-dimensional Earth realms rather than from space. Few humans seeking the New Age realize this, giving all the credit to outer space contact.

We are confused by the fact that while humans perceive their own planet's natural environment as beautiful, they assume nature spirits are childish and mostly not highly evolved. Humans also assume that beings from a far distant planet never experienced by humans, are very wise and evolved. It is true that there are very low frequencies of energy on Earth, but do they come from nature or from human beings?

It may seem like a minor point in these hectic days of change, but it is urgent that those gentle, good people who seek the light, and who are the spiritual warriors of the Change Times, no longer hold onto the old belief that nature spirits or other "earthly energy" is automatically less evolved.

Nature has infinite wisdom to bestow on humankind. She will gladly do this, gladly give this gift to her child, if only humankind will open ears, eyes, hearts, and soul, to her.

The Creator Spirit is a female energy as well as a male energy. Who holds the key to creation? The male of the species holds half of it. But the female holds the miracle of birthing and nourishing creation. This knowledge must come into every heart and soul. My transmission closes now as the sun sets on this day.

With love for all creation,
Naomi

To complete the "Threat From Mother Nature" section, we will give an extraterrestrial the last word. She is "Amethysta" whom we hear from often in our **Change Times Quarterly**. A friend of ours first met Amethysta during a face to face encounter with her; Amethysta's starcraft (UFO) had landed in the snow and our friend witnessed Amethysta and her crewmates emerge from the craft to investigate and enjoy the cold white stuff!

I then started hearing from Amethysta telepathically. I see her as my friend described her physically, a very small alien with large eyes, a large head, and a face which tapers to a very small chin. She is childlike in many ways but also very wise, seeming also like a little old lady.

Recently Amethysta sent this message to me:

"...I do not aim to sound depressing, but I want to give you an accurate picture of how urgent it is that we (and you) communicate with, and heal, the Mother Planet.

She is not my mother world but I love Terra; she is unique in the universe and her blue/green image is always a welcome one from the viewscreen of my starcraft.

My home planet knows and loves her well, because I often communicate with the spirit of my home world, and she tells me these things.

Gaia Is Desperate

I also have the ability to communicate clearly with Gaia, the spirit of Earth, and I know her desperation. I know the signals which go out from her, toward my home world and toward her other planetary colleagues across the universe.

She doubts she can make it through. Chaos seems imminent and even sounds like a relief to her at times. She is tired of trying to hold things together, of struggling to survive and be gentle when humankind keeps destroying more and more of her.

It is difficult to go on, for instance, when your immune system is badly damaged; many humans now sadly know this truth.

I stress that all is not lost yet. There is still hope that we (you and us), can save her. Indeed, we *are*, little by little. We are supplying her with reason to go on, with just that little bit of love, cleansing, and healing, which is necessary for any of us to keep going. She does not require a great deal to keep going because she is a world supercharged with lust for life!

To pull her through, we need to give her more, to make our commitment to saving her an even greater part of our lives. We extraterrestrials can no longer afford to sit back and help from afar; we will be coming closer to Earth, becoming more involved.

Our time of advising from the safety of the skies above, is over.

The threat Mother Nature now poses to herself and her lifeforms is because of her anger and desperation. Spiritually ease these terrible emotions, and you will move a step closer to surviving yourself. Plus, you will have helped save a world.

Gaian energies are absolutely amazing and magical to work with. Of course I relate easiest to my own planet, but of all other worlds, I find Earth to be the most fascinating. I love to work with her. As a human, you must be very proud of your Mother World.

In unconditional love and eternal light,

I AM Amethysta

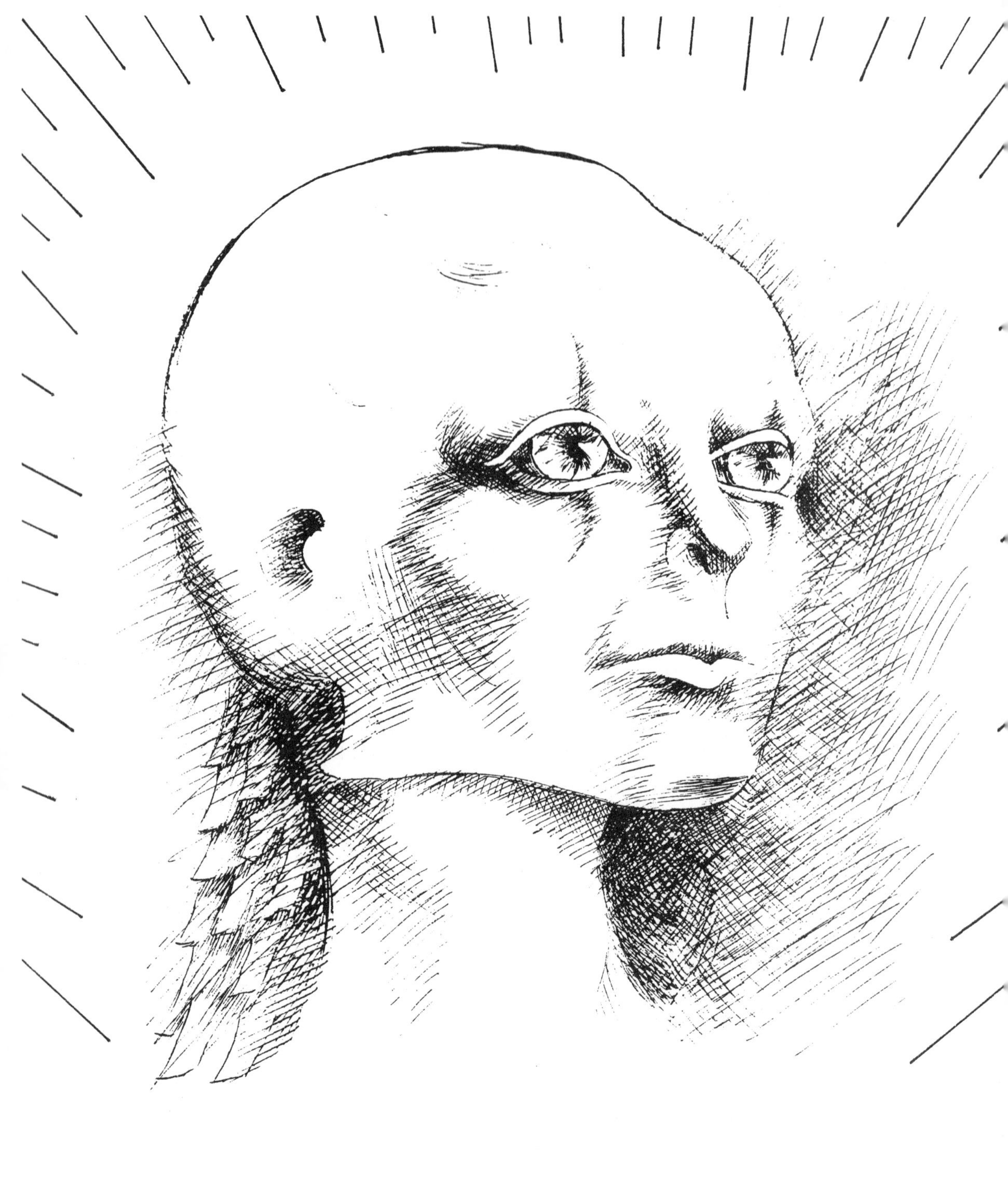

Amethysta came to Merrilie telepathically and directed her as to her physical appearance. Artist: Merrilie Miller.

THE THREAT OF OVER-POPULATION

This is Tibus. I come to you in Love and Light.

Diane, you have asked me to explain our viewpoint on human overpopulation in these last few years of the Twentieth Century, because you recognize that this is one of the gravest threats facing the planet.

I have told you before that being able to perceive and adapt to "paradox" is a key to surviving The Change Times, and then, to flourishing in a new, higher dimension.

I won't go rambling about the intricacies of "paradox" at this moment, but essentially I wish to state that the overpopulation of Earth is a paradox.

There are too many human beings on the planet, billions "too many," for the Mother Planet to support.

On the other hand, the new, higher dimension will not emerge unless that sad fact is true.

The Synergy of Change

In this way, there is a synergy between the energy of a living, changing, evolving reality and the billions of consciousnesses (humans) within it.

To put it another way, the Change Point would not occur if there were ten people living on the planet. The more people there are, the more it forces the leap in consciousness into a higher dimension.

Paradoxes are really annoying commodities because they force one to say things like, "It is both good and bad that Earth is so over-populated."

It is not just severe overpopulation which causes the dilemma and has this paradoxical quality. Almost every piece of evidence which proves that Earth's Change Times is happening now, is paradoxical in nature.

It is tragic that the Mother Planet has been raped and pillaged by her own child (humankind), but if humankind had not strayed so far from decency and reverence, the new love for the Mother Planet which exists among enlightened people like you, would never have happened. Of course you would love nature, but you would not feel the urgency and therefore not study, meditate, and sharpen your spiritual/psychic skills in so many ways. You would not rediscover your ancient link to her, so sacred and dynamic.

As we have mentioned before, every planet with intelligent life goes through a "Change Times" and a "Change Point" therein. From this point, the planet either evolves into a new, enlightened world with higher awareness, or perishes.

The "intelligent life" on the planet is what/whom decides the fate of the planet. This is because this "intelligent life" has developed technology which will destroy the planet, and they have predictably gotten out of touch spiritually with their Mother Planet. The big test is whether they can abandon the evil technology and sophistication, and get back in touch with their planet's spirituality (which is also their own).

Some planets who have perished are completely lifeless; some have been blown from orbit and the dead mass of the planet is no longer there. Other planets who did not make it, have a semblance of life such as micro-organisms, fungus, perhaps insects such as cockroaches and occasionally mammals such as rats. (Keep in mind, other planets may not have had mammals but we are explaining this in Earth terms).

The Change Point is a huge gamble for a planet, a terrible risk-taking. Humanity did not realize it was bringing this process about when it so badly abused the planet, but Gaia herself, on some level of consciousness, knew this was bound to happen. Her knowledge and wisdom span the universe, because she is one in a family of billions of planets and stars.

The Language of the Planets

These planet entities exchange wisdom and knowledge, they communicate with each other. They commune with each other. Who is to say that the sounds which scientists record coming from deep space are not communications from one world to another, the voices of planets?

Even though Earth knew on some level of consciousness that she, like all worlds, was bound to face a Change Times, this knowledge does not stop her from agonizing and hurting as this phase of her existence actually takes place. It is something like a female giving birth; she knows the actual birth will hurt, knows this fact since she first learned the facts of life. But how can she avoid this?

She cannot, if she is to be a mother someday. If she dies at birth, it is tragic. If she manages to give birth to new life and then survive and recover herself, it is all worth it. She happily looks back on it, glad it is over.

Planets approach their time of crisis in a psychologically similar way. The "intelligent race" threatens to extinguish all life, and the Mother World suffers. That "intelligent race" must then become really intelligent and evolve, spiritually, emotionally, and psychically. New life is born!

Overpopulation of the dominant species is very common as a world approaches its Change Point. It all seems to boil down to: Is all the suffering to be worth it? Will some (even just a few), members of the dominant species lead the world into a higher frequency? Or is all the suffering to be for nothing, and the world dies? In the process of the Change Times, the population almost always is cut back through natural catastrophe and other disasters.

You are watching the worst part of childbirth as these Change Times ensue. The miracle has not yet happened. You must not only hear Gaia's screams, but you must know it is up to you (and those like you), to make the birth successful. No wonder you find daily life difficult. But, a miracle awaits!

Choose the best of all possible realities, then aim your consciousness right at that mark on the Reality Continuum. And help give birth to a new and better world. Raise the frequency!

May the healing light of God and goodness surround you, always,
Tibus

THE THREAT FROM TECHNOLOGY

This is Veritan. I come to you in the light of logic and intelligence.

Science fiction and science speculation is a cherished creation of the human mind, and also, from the universal mind (after all, they are one and the same).

Science fiction and speculation is the ability to throw one's mind into branch realities, or at least, to perceive the possibility of a branch reality which does not currently exist.

The possible future, negative or positive, or a possible alternate reality (dimension), is based on what is currently plausible and logical (thus the "science" half of "science fiction").

We have channeled messages to you in the past about Star Trek, Star Wars, and other science fiction as being possible windows on the future, or on another Earth reality. They are a way of preparing humans for what will be. And, they are a way of actually creating the future. I do not wish to make that subject the focus of this channeling, but I do hope you will ponder this concept.

The subject of this channeling is computers, and the probable threat they pose to humankind. Science fiction stories have often featured computers which have become "too smart," and which have gained a sense of self-awareness (consciousness). Perhaps the most famous of these is HAL in the book and film 2001, A Space Odyssey.

The subject of artificial intelligence is one which we of Space/Dimensional Intelligence, grapple with constantly. No, we do not have it all figured out. There are many involved in trying to save Earth who *chose* centuries ago, not to have "machines" in their realities at all. These are the light forms, those of the angelic realms. We commend them for living as advanced, free-energy life forms.

But in another way, one must also commend those of us who in our bumbling corporeal way, grapple with questions rather than floating above them. Humans tend to categorize, feeling that angels are the most advanced while those in space who are still in corporeal form, such as humanoid aliens, are not as good or as advanced.

However, we do not have this need to "tag" each other. An angelic being does not feel he or she is superior to a humanoid alien. And I do not feel I am "better" just because I do grapple with the problems of the physical world. All of us have accepted long ago that we all have struggles and achievements to be proud of, and that the common denominator is love. We all respect other lifeforms as equal.

Computers Threaten All Life

Since humans are much involved in the physical and technical world, I am transmitting this message on computers as they now threaten the planet. The threat is real and great. I will leave aside the argument as to whether artificial intelligence is in itself a negative creation, or if it can sometimes be positive.

Humans are entering the dawn of creating true artificial intelligence. Machine consciousness. This sends chills through anyone who reads the many science fiction and speculation books which present a world where computers control humans.

In the Eastern Hemisphere, they are approaching machine intelligence through software, whereas in the West, they are approaching it through actual computers (hardware) as the source of consciousness/intelligence.

Either way, this step is revolutionary one and ranks with the discovery of atomic power as marking the planet's entrance into a new era. No planet will ever be the same once nuclear power is unleashed, and no planet is ever the same after computers/machines gain self-awareness.

The third revolutionary step which happens to every planet is that no planet will ever be the same after the process of life is tampered with, such as gene-splicing, cloning, and controlled genetics.

These are the three major elements of The Change Times in technical terms. And they are the three main technical threats.

Computers gaining self-awareness and possibly wanting to control humanity, even if this is what is "best" for humanity in the computer's estimation, is the most pressing technical threat to life on Earth. This has replaced the nuclear threat as the most likely possibility.

Already you know how a computer error can wreck havoc in your life. Computers already control whether you have food on the table. That is, when you pay for food with check or credit card, a computer says whether you can have your groceries. And "cash" will soon be a thing of the past.

Who among you does not wonder about the government's computer list of "subversives" who are highly interested in UFOs and psychic phenomenon?

But these computers are not self aware, self righteous, nor self enforcing, yet!

The fact is, Earth scientist are three years away from reconstructing the intelligence of a cat in the artificial intelligence of a computer. This in itself is a travesty of natural law, and we shudder to think of the "test animals" involved in the research.

However, to move beyond the ethical and moral considerations for a moment, we must realize that a cat shows emotion and a very strong will power. A cat makes decisions and is very much its own boss. A cat shows loves, and hate. Can you imagine a computer with these traits?

And to look at this in a spiritual light, a cat has a soul, that unique energy which binds all natural life to the Creator. It is that "special stuff" which energizes all natural beings, with the blessings of the Creator. A computer has no such binding, no such soul.

Computer Takeover In Ten Years

If the technical age were to continue, computers and robots would take over the world in ten to twenty years. Without souls, would there be any doubt that they would feel human life, and other natural lifeforms, to be completely inferior and expendable? They would create more of themselves and "the creator" (humankind), would no longer be needed.

Science fiction? At this moment, there are machines on Earth which can *learn.* Sometimes they respond in an entirely different way than scientists expect.

However, you may be saying that The Change Times is in effect. Is it then a blessing that the natural disasters and eventual dimensional change, will stop artificial intelligence dead in its tracks?

It will be stopped "dead," if events of The Change Times are very drastic. If civilization is destroyed, technology will be gone, or nearly gone. But if a kinder reality is brought about, and things are not-that-bad (let's say, a "3" on the Reality Continuum), then such research will survive.

Does this mean that we should all work for an absolute end to civilization, so that research into artificial intelligence, nuclear fusion, cloning, and gene splicing is utterly destroyed?

No, of course not. We all know that frequency (the level of consciousness), will be higher when we bring The Change Times into a bright new dimension. This level of spiritual integrity is the only thing which will stop scientists from pursuing frightening and dangerous fields of research.

Or, if this research is continued in the new, higher frequency, it will be done with great caution and spiritual integrity, and intelligence. As it is now, it is being done with no spiritual integrity, no intelligence. They is simply urged to go ahead, full speed.

Incidentally, my planet managed to survive its Change Point and keep technology, too. We summoned our spiritual integrity and intelligence, and we kept computers and machines, being careful that they never got power over us. And, making certain we did not victimize any lifeform (such as the cat), to further our research.

Artificial intelligence is still the subject of ongoing debate among us. But we have overcome the threat it posed in raw form.

We have examined this aspect of a planet's spiritual evolution process, and we have examined it personally and painfully. We concluded long ago that the only hope when a planet embarks on a technical course which is minus spiritual and moral integrity, is to raise the spiritual frequency.

If it does not raise the frequency, Earth is doomed through the above mentioned "machine" threats in a very few years, even without natural disasters, overpopulation, and viral epidemics.

Why am I transmitting this message to you when you have no physical control over what research scientists are doing?

I wish to increase the urgency you feel to bring about a rise in frequency!

If you feel slightly complacent that Earth can just slide into the 21st Century as is, it is my duty to tell you that these machine/science dangers lie just up the road, in ten or twenty years. These are dangers you have not yet begun to comprehend, or deal with. And it is a very real danger that by the time you do comprehend and deal with it will be too late. Therefore, I am trying to awaken you "early!"

These technical dangers lie there waiting, in a branch of reality. But the raising of the spiritual frequency can and will diffuse these dangers. A better alternate branch of reality will have then been chosen. This is the only action on humanity's part which can diffuse this danger.

Dimensional Change Is the Answer

These science fiction-like threats to all life on Earth can only be avoided through dimensional change in the latter days of the 20th Century. This point is the window of opportunity. It will have closed twenty years up the road.

I give you this picture so that you have a more precise idea of what you are working for, and what you are fighting against. The emphasis of our work is usually centered on Nature and the Cosmos. But you must be fully aware of the other side of the coin in order to fight and overcome its power.

Satan Reveals Himself

If there is such an entity as Satan, it reveals itself in technical nightmares and machines-gone-mad. I do not see any evidence of Satan in anything natural, be it a fascinating little black bat, a beautiful, sleek black cat, or even a dark and thundering wind storm.

But might Satan be a computer which/who gained self-awareness and ego, and then attempts to make itself ruler over humankind? After all, when humans cast themselves in the role of The Creator, instead of leaving that role to God, then perhaps humans can only create "Satan," a soulless entity with no spiritual binding to God.

Perhaps I am getting carried away. Perhaps we can hide this transmission from Tibus who will chuckle and say I just proved all his points against computers. Usually I defend their logic, their lack of scrambled, confusing emotion, and their efficiency. It is time I stopped transmitting for now!

In infinite care and empathy,

I AM Veritan.

THE THREAT FROM NUCLEAR ENERGY

We must include channeled information on the nuclear threat.

In our first book, **The Transformation** Tibus told us that this energy, unleashed, and other technical nightmares, are Satan, or as close to Satan as we would ever come.

He spoke of dimensional rips occurring if there were nuclear war. These rips threatened other dimensions as well as our own earthly one. Now in the preceding channeling, Veritan has confirmed this viewpoint; perhaps The Devil was not created at all by The Creator, but is human-made. Technical. Given birth by scientists who have no spiritual or moral integrity.

It is true that The Creator created humankind, so perhaps in that indirect way, The Creator also created the evil technical threats of which we speak. If this is true, we there are two truths which emerge:

One is that humankind must return to The Creator's vision.

The link must be re-energized and purified, through connecting to the Mother Planet, and to The Cosmos once more. We must consciously celebrate this link!

Two is that we must make a new positive reality out of the technical evils which threaten us, by learning our lesson as a race! If we can learn the lesson, it has all been worth it! If we do not, Evil and Oblivion await. After all, "Evil" and "Oblivion" are one and the same commodity. *Life* is everything. With Oblivion, all is lost including the soul.

I received the following transmission from Tibus at a time in 1992 when a nuclear leak had been discovered at Sosnovy Bor, a nuclear installation near St. Petersburg in Russia. I have received many transmissions on Chernobyl and other nuclear installations, throughout the years; several of these transmissions turned out to be prophetic regarding leaks and shut downs of specific installations.

While the radiation leak at Sosnovy Bor was harnessed, we feel Tibus' words apply in a more general way, even today:

This is Tibus. I come to you in love and light.

The radiation leak at Sosnovy Bor is worse than reported, but it is not as bad as Chernobyl. The area around St. Petersburg is relatively heavily populated and more measures should have been taken to protect the population. Although, it is tragically nearly impossible to protect the populace from radiation once it has been leaked. There is a chance that this particular leak will reoccur because it has not been repaired completely. As things stand now, radiation from Sosnovy Bor poses no threat to as wide an area as Chernobyl did (and still does).

Certainly all nuclear installations in the former U.S.S.R. are in bad repair. There are also many installations in the U.S. and elsewhere which are dangerous. I have sent urgent messages before regarding Sellafield Nuclear Plant in Britain. I repeat this warning!

Abandon Nuclear Energy!

This form of energy is no good. The human race must move away from it. Now!

The details of Sosnovy Bor have been censored, kept from the media and from the people of the world. The source of this censorship is not Russia, as you might think, but rather the European Union. We have given other warnings regarding the European Union, how it is being and will be, misused by those greedy for power.

The EU's censorship of a radiation leak in Russia may sound illogical but it is not when one perceives the plans for "The New World Order." These plans are being carried out by those who are power-hungry and who wish to control the finances of the entire world. They do not care if their own people are contaminated by radiation, and they certainly do not care if humans, animals, and the environment are victims of radiation poisoning worldwide. They have their secret underground bunkers to protect them from radioactivity.

When the U.S.S.R. fell apart, a power vacuum was created. This vacuum attracts power hungry politicians, financial experts, and ruthless military men from other countries and cartels. Their allegiance is to no country or tribe, only to themselves.

Consider for a moment the mountains of scientific research and the military arsenal which was the U.S.S.R. Its people stood in long lines for bread while no expense was spared in developing weapons and technical innovations. What became of this vast wealth of weapons, research, and other scientific/technical "jewels?"

Tibus as he appears psychically to artist Merrilie Miller.

These were not split up among the small nationalistic republics as people were told. They were sold to individuals, some within the United States.

It is actually a benefit to these power hungry individuals to allow nuclear plants such as Sosnovy Bor to deteriorate. It is to the benefit of these power hungry individuals to allow chaos to reign politically, wherever possible. Remember, they owe allegiance to no country.

The concept of the balance of power is an important one. When balance is lost between superpowers, a vacuum is created and the situation becomes very dangerous. Opportunists with only their ow self-interests, rush in to fill the vacuum. The superpower government still intact also gains all the scientific and technical knowledge of the failed superpower. This also serves self interests and power hungry individuals. The temptation is too great. "Absolute power corrupts, absolutely."

At this moment in the historical timeline, the power hungry feel they are close to achieving "ultimate power."

Governments and ESP Research

For instance, the former Soviet Union did a lot of research in extrasensory perception, psychic powers, and the paranormal.

If the greedy individuals within the E.U. or the U.S. can gain full possession of this research, they know they can save billions of dollars (they think only in money terms). They feel they can inherit this research without having invested in it. The temptation is irresistible to them.

As well as individuals within the E.U. and the U.S. manipulating this research, there are also smaller cartels and very wealthy individuals trying to come into possession of the full body of psi research from the U.S.S.R.

This is worse than when the U.S.S.R. was a functioning entity because then where was a balance of power.

With one group of individuals in control of the full body of psi research, all weapons and warfare are obsolete. However, the completion of this Soviet psi research was fortunately stalled a few years ago, partially because of lack of funds, and partially because then President Gorbachev questioned the morality of such research.

However, it would take but a little research to complete several earthshaking projects in the psi field. These could alter what is perceived as reality, but alter it in a deceptive, false way. The implications are enormous regarding this threat which is basically a technical one (not pure psychic power on its own), from a field called psychotronics.

(The rest of this transmission was received in 1996 from Tibus, but it is dealing with the same subject):

It is always difficult to transmit information concerning the world political/military establishment and then to answer the question, "Well, what can I as one small individual, do about it?"

Enlightened people everywhere are willing to help, but how, when such huge powers and powerful individuals are involved?

Certainly this is one area where your psychic meditation can and will help!

One must work on raising the frequencies of those in positions of great power and wealth. They must begin to question the morality of seeking absolute power and wealth.

Nuclear Installations In Bad Repair

Many nuclear installations across the globe are in bad shape and we must reach those in power through spiritual wavelengths, and beg them to repair the plants, or shut them down. Maybe this sounds simplistic to you, maybe you feel those in power will never change. But molecules of consciousness are indeed affected by other molecules of consciousness. You can reach their minds and souls in this way. Evil individuals are not 100% evil, they can be mellowed and changed. We are attempting to speed this mellowing process up by giving them "strange experiences" such as UFO sightings and visitations. President Gorbachev experienced these things, became inspired, and may have saved the world – for the moment! This effort to reach leaders them is not as hopeless as you might skeptically think. They can be reached, and changed.

In the field of psychic warfare, leaders must be scared into not using it, that is, scared if that is the only course of action left. We can see to it that this "terrible fright" happens to these power hungry individuals. This we can promise you. The same fate awaits those who would go ahead with nuclear war.

If The New World Order continues, it will end in global disaster. But if we can stop it, it will have gone onward just long enough to teach the lesson, "This must never happened again!"

There is little that enlightened individuals can do except reach the greedy "leaders" (they are not true leaders), through

spiritual and psychic wavelength. You can knock physically on their doors but they are inaccessible, guarded by squads of security men. They do not listen much to "popular movements" so joining an antinuclear group is good for your soul, and it doesn't hurt to add to the numbers opposing nuclear energy, but this effort most likely will not reach these evil individuals.

Psychically, you can reach them directly, personally. Their walls do not hold back your spiritual thrust.

Becoming A Spiritual Warrior

This is one of many ways you can be a spiritual warrior.

I am telling you now that spiritually aware people do not fully realize the power of their collective spiritual voice!

Even as individuals, your telepathic powers are great. Your psi potential is just beginning and can be developed greatly in a short period of time.

We would not expect you to telepathically give these greedy individuals specific, detailed thoughts because that is much harder to do telepathically, and this could be considered interference in another's inner space. To give you an extreme example, a telepathically gifted person would be wrong to send the fatal message, to one of the power hungry individuals who are attempting to run the world: "Walk over to the balcony. Now jump off."

However, you can send the frequency of love, of sensitivity, and of empathy for others to the power-hungry so that they do develop spiritually, a regard for life. One does not need an exact location for the individual you are reaching telepathically. You do not even need to know their names, because many of the power-hungry individuals are unknown names (they wish to have it this way).

What you do know is their aspirations, you know how ambitious they are to hold ultimate power and to have "all" the money. You can find them telepathically through this description; telepathy seldom uses names and addresses anyway. Telepathy works conceptually. Think of these greedy individuals as actors in a play, and telepathically reach their archetypical role in the universal play of life.

I leave you now, with the promise of my guidance, protection, and universal love.

May the healing light of God and goodness surround you, always,
Tibus

In another channeling about the evils of nuclear energy, Tibus addresses nuclear testing by large governments:

This is Tibus. I come to you in love and light.

One of the variables we worry most about, is the possibility of a government/military group, through nuclear testing or other high-energy testing, providing the trigger which causes "The Big One" (earthquake) or other natural disaster. We worry about this because it is one of the least controllable factors.

Mother Nature is a lot more cooperative than governments are, and we do not need to worry about The Noninterference Directive when communicating directly with the Mother Planet.

Earthquakes are normal for the planet, but huge quakes are not, at this stage in her life. When she was young, she did have "temper tantrums" which manifested as huge earthquakes. I realize, incidentally, that there is also a scientific explanation for this, but science and my more mystical language do not contradict each other. On up the road, science and mysticism meet. They are two halves of a whole, two refreshing ways of perceiving the same reality.

However, now Earth is a middle-aged planet. She would not grow insanely violent (huge earthquakes) unless she simply loses patience with the damage done to her and the disregard shown for her life and welfare by humankind.

But, government/military nuclear testing could trigger a huge quake which would have been otherwise a middle-sized one.

Telepathically Reaching the Greedy

Our enlightened friends have a good chance of reaching greedy, power-hungry individuals telepathically but it is difficult to reach an entire government and change its policy toward nuclear testing. Recently we on the Home Side have attempted to telepathically reach the French government which continues above ground nuclear testing in the Pacific Ocean, thus endangering the native people who live there, and the ecology of both land (islands) and water (ocean). We had some success for a while, but then the policy of testing above ground continued. Remember, we cannot/would not practice absolute mind control, thus we can only attempt to influence to the positive.

Gaia, the spirit of Earth, on the other hand, is a delightful natural, psychic creature, and she can be reached telepathically very easily. It is she who gave birth to the psychic gift which exists in all lifeforms of this planet. When you reach her psychically, you are talking her language. And so we beg you once again to work with her psychically. Calm her anger, ease her pain, heal her.

Governments are artificial bodies built completely within the mundane frequency; these are not, as I have said, prone to being reached through psychic meditation. If governments were to become enlightened, they would have to do away with themselves! (Remember, power hungry individuals are a different matter and can be reached psychically).

All in all, we can only reaffirm the fact that we must raise the frequency so that such evil and self-serving governments, with their huge military establishments, become extinct. Their methods of doing and ways of operating will be so alien in the risen frequency, that they simply cannot and will not exist, even for a microsecond.

The same is true of the "money system" which holds the human race captive. It is outmoded and causes more harm than good. A few greedy individuals horde all they can while the common person has none, or very little. The split between "the rich and the poor" grows wider each day. The middle class which once was the dominant class in the U.S. is nearly gone. It is unthinkable to us on the Home Side, that people cannot get proper medical attention because of the evil stuff, "money." The list is endless of similar injustices under the present system which worships "money."

It is truly time for a new way of thinking, acting, feeling, and being! It is time to evolve, to undergo a miraculous transformation into cosmic citizenship. The human race has taken other major steps in evolution in the past, just as other species have. We know you can do it.

Now is the time for a major leap in spiritual evolution! Soon it will be too late. We are here to help you make this leap. Join us, take our hands, and you will take a step upward on the awareness ladder.

May the healing light of God and goodness surround you always,

Tibus

Diane and her dogs, Sinsee and Diva, enjoying Mother Nature in the Comeragh Mountains of County Tipperary, Ireland.

CHAPTER TEN: UFO OCCUPANTS: COME ON DOWN!

One thing I have learned in my long association with Tibus and his friends is that they are as diverse as you can possibly imagine, and then some!

Star Trek has a wonderful, wise slogan: "Infinite Diversity in Infinite Combinations!" The Vulcans worship this belief which they call "IDIC" because they celebrate diversity, feeling that this aspect of the universe is, in itself, a tremendous positive.

We as a human race have yet to learn this lesson. We hate each other because we are a slightly lighter or darker color, because our nostrils are slightly more or less spread, because we talk the same language with a slightly different "twang." We hate each other because we are Christian, but one belongs to a Protestant branch while another belongs to a Catholic branch. How infinitesimal is this difference when viewed from outer space! The list of our petty bickerings is endless based on the fact that we perceive another to be "different."

IDIC is yet another example of Star Trek's implanted vision, because Tibus and his friends of Space/Dimensional Intelligence do indeed rejoice in, and celebrate, the infinite diversity which is out there in the galaxy, and the universe beyond. They see us as the human race; our many cultures make us fascinating, a truly creative and imaginative race, full of curiosity.

The life spark manifests in so many forms. The Creator Spirit has a magnificent imagination indeed. If we doubt this, we have only to look at the variety of lifeforms on Earth. Or, taking an example from my own environment, we have only to look at the diversity of lifeforms here in the High Desert of California. How miraculous that lifeforms adapt to adverse conditions such as exist here! Those adaptations might make them look a bit comical, like the roadrunner in my back yard, but they are proven survivors.

Meeting Alien Friends

In my channeling, I have heard from a delightful variety of extraterrestrials and other-dimensional beings. Since I am an experienced psychic and channeler, and since Tibus protects me quite well anyway, I have never heard from a frightening or extremely negative being. Sometimes the entity from whom I receive a telepathic message, is very alien indeed. In those cases, I have been known to feel slightly disoriented or mind-boggled, but I soon adjust. I often feel that the alien is as disoriented and mind-boggled by me as I am by him or her. I remember, for instance, the first time Veritan channeled through; he was very confused and apologetic, like a child trying to learn the levers of a new toy.

But I can truthfully say that I have never "met" a member of the Space/Time Intelligence who is not an inspirational and good soul. Gentle. Empathetic. Loving. Concerned.

Someday, I know that myself and others, will meet these same aliens face to face. I await this meeting eagerly! I will feel great excitement, and I hope to have a grasp of the enormity of what is transpiring, but I will honestly have no fear. I know these individuals already, their hearts and souls. I know they are of good intent. I like them very much, from the inside, out.

This is one of the goals of the alien/human channeling phenomenon: To acquaint some humans intimately with the alien vibration so that there will not be fear in face to face meetings. We who channel can help others also, to not run scared when face to face meetings occur, as they will. And then, we will work together!

I urge those of you who do feel some fear of the unknown, and at the thought of meeting aliens face to face, to embark on psychic contact with them. I will give you some special contact meditations later in the book.

Your Personal Guardian

Each of you reading these words does have a special contact who is gentle, loving, and enlightened. He or she may be your guardian angel or your star guardian from the Space/Dimensional group. Or, you may have a special contact in the Spirit World, a loving relative or friend who has passed on. There is someone "out there" who will guide you safely on your mission of psychic contact. They will protect you from negative energies and entities.

You will also want to prepare yourself by washing yourself in the golden white light of unconditional love and goodness first. We will tell you how to do this later on.

Now, I would like to have you meet some of the alien friends we have encountered through our **Change Times Quarterly** and through **The Star Network Heartline** our monthly newsletter.

Surviving these days of Earth Changes means being able to meet beings from other worlds and other dimensions. If you cannot do this, you will be stuck in a dimension which is unravelling and falling apart because of natural catastrophes, viral epidemics, high technology gone mad, and sweeping climate changes.

You must be with the group of enlightened humans who are able to move on to a new intersect point on the Reality Continuum. In other words, you must engineer a new reality. The power of your mind can create a new reality base, an alternate reality to the one which is crumbling. This is basic metaphysics and this is also quantum physics. It can be done!

In this new, risen frequency, there are universal beings, not just humans. They come from the other dimensions of Earth as well as from planets in outer space. They come from Time itself, because the new dimension accepts the fact that time travel is possible and is, in fact, a reality. Remember that Time *is* dimension.

No longer will the reducing valve of your mind "censor out" realities such as time travel, angels, starships, and extraterrestrials. At long last, you will be open to all the universe has to offer, you will be able to perceive a million advanced, wonderful beings and places which have been kept from you thus far.

Will you be up to this?

Let's begin by meeting an ancient tribe called **The Tuatha De Danann.** Their name is in the Irish language; in English it means "The Family of Diane."

This tribe lived in Ireland and other parts of Europe long before the time of Christ. The legend is that they came from the sky, being very beautiful and intelligent people. They settled on Earth and gave us many psychic secrets and advanced knowledge. But let's let them tell their own story.

We are the Tuatha De Danann. We are beings of The Light and we send love and blessings to all who read these words.

Before The Great Pyramid was constructed, before Stonehenge was erected in its first incarnation (it has been changed and re-built by several later tribes), and before the Greek and Roman civilizations flourished, we roamed freely on Earth.

It was we who built Newgrange in Country Meath, Ireland. We urge you to educate yourself about Newgrange if you are lacking this information, because this astronomical observatory and sacred temple is 1,000 years older than The Great Pyramid in Egypt. It holds many profound truths for seekers of The Light today.

We disappeared into a safe dimension, a secure level of existence, when humankind veered from Mother Nature's path, and thus from God's intent. We are fond of saying that we turned "sideways to the sun." We are still here, we are still real and solid, but you cannot normally perceive us.

However, we will soon be back in the world you know, not to take it from you, not to conquer, but to share, to help, to learn, to heal, to teach. There is much you can give us as well. And when we say, "We will be back in your world," we might just as accurately say, "You will be evolving into our world."

We knew we would be together with you again someday, when the mundane dimension which we can no longer bear, is about to give way to a higher frequency, which is like home to us.

The world you know was our home since before recorded history. That was before the "mundane frequency" became the dominant way of thinking, feeling, and being. Our days on your Earth were as "Eden," to use one of your terms.

Greed Became God

But then, greed became god in the human race's reality. Power became king. And, we left. We were hurt and dejected, seeing what humankind had made of himself.

But we did not leave. That is not a contradiction. We stayed with our Mother Planet but we did not stay in your physical world.

During the millennia when we lived in our other-dimensional refuge, we encountered space aliens who had the means to travel to other Earth dimensions as well as to the physical Earth plane (mundane dimension). Since we came from the sky, according to our own legends, we felt kindred to these extraterrestrials who were dimensional travelers like us.

However, some of these aliens proved not to be of The Light. There were battles with them, battles more of mind and soul than physical battles. We soon found that the positive space aliens were more than friends, they were brothers and sisters to us in our battle to rid our other-dimensional refuge of the negative aliens who had gotten a foothold there.

The positive extraterrestrials fought our battles with us and often guided and protected us. We sometimes could do the same for them. It was/is a great alliance, a linkage. Love arose between us.

Today, you can hardly tell us apart and for this, we rejoice!

We are The Tuatha De Danann, ending transmission for now.

You can imagine my surprise one day when I heard from "*Lita*" who is an extraterrestrial member of the Space/Dimensional Intelligence. Lita has genetic roots in the lizard (reptoid) group. Her vibrations were very strange to me, but not unpleasant.

I only heard from her once, but she had an important message for us, and I was emotionally touched by her presence.

This is Lita. You don't know me but I do come in peace and in a positive vibration.

Look within yourself, and if your heart and intuition don't agree with my words, then just turn me off. Please do not feel I am criticizing humans and humanoids in an unjust way, but I feel I have a legitimate complaint and I speak for a number of other lifeforms as well.

Please be careful when you who call yourselves "channels" are receiving transmissions, do not impose your preconceived concepts upon "raw" communications you receive.

You receive such communications in telepathic, conceptual form and an individual who has the gift for channeling is capable of changing these telepathic concepts into "language" which others understand. But the transmission filters through your mind, too, and it is here that human prejudices can become superimposed on the original message.

Do you realize that the current scenario which is believed by many New Agers and other parties interested in UFOs, projects that human-like aliens are the good guys and the less-human "little grey creatures" are the bad guys ? This is assumed in an all encompassing way. There is not the perception, "We must judge each individually."

Judge The Reptoids Individually

It has now developed, according to some channels, that "the really bad aliens" are a race of reptiles, often called, "The Reptoids." They are said to be moving toward Earth to conquer it, enslave all humans, and possibly have them for dinner.

You humans evolved physically from the ape race, and I am a life form who evolved physically from a lizard race. I object to your stereotypical role designations and I emphasize that I am not coming to conquer or eat you. This is the kind of primitive thinking which the New Age does not need.

Can't you humans be more creative than to come up with echoes of the same old human chauvinism which has wrecked your planet? Hitler was not reptilian, nor are the other greedy individuals who are attempting to become omnipotent today. They were/are humans!

We nonhumanoids have a right to be frightened of the human race, look how many of us you have murdered through mindless hunting and uncaring antiecological policies. Can you say the same thing has happened to humans, or humanoids, at the hands of lizard people?

Why then, do you blindly accept that a race of reptiles is chugging toward Earth to enslave and eat humanity? I suppose fast starships which do not ever "chug" are only occupied by humans and humanoids? We reptiles must have out of date ships like some old Klingon vessel in Star Trek.

I am not telling you that negative aliens do not exist, because they do, and they have performed scientific experiments on humans. This is as sad and wrong as when a human performs a scientific experiment on any other lifeform, or on another human being.

It is also true that Earth militaries are working with negative aliens, and have in the past. Some of these negative aliens are of a grey race but many are not. How prejudiced it is, then, for UFOlogists and New Agers to refer to "the greys" with inherent negativity attached. This is the same as referring to "the blacks" or "the yellows" as being the all-negative groups on Earth. Indeed, if one race has done more than its share of damage, it is the white race.

Could it be that films such as Close Encounters of the Third Kind and E.T. engendered in humanity a deep love for the small grey alien?

Therefore, did "the powers that be" start a disinformation campaign emphasizing the "evil" of this group? Did militaries and the governments they serve conclude that humankind was about to move forward spiritually, leaving their governments behind and powerless? The link which was forming between positive greys and humans has been damaged effectively.

Beware of Disinformation!

I stress that I am not denying the "evil alien scientist" scenario; however, I do know that there has been much disinformation from both channels and from governments. One example is that, "All greys work for a terribly bad race of reptiles." This is blatantly untrue and is the kind of cheap science fiction which humanity must leave behind as it seeks its new, higher place in the galaxy. The New Age is not about weaving science fiction stories. If one wishes to do this, he or she should become a science fiction author.

The real blame belongs to Earth governments who have allowed themselves to go into "partnership" with negative aliens, some of whom look entirely human. From this has come the infamous UFO abductions where humans are used in scientific experiments, mostly of a genetic nature. These are absolutely wrong and should not happen. Still, the big threat to billions of humans is not from these experiments, but rather from natural catastrophes, viral epidemics, climate change, overpopulation, and human technology careening out of control.

Humans must overcome chauvinistic tendencies. In human mythology, beautiful superhumans are the heros, while animal-like creatures (especially the lowly reptile), is the archetypical villain. In these days of copious space channeling, humans can better accept that a ball of light is the hero than a lizard-looking individual.

I only ask that next time you encounter a stately iguana in the zoo (a species endangered by humans), or a small chameleon, that you see if you can feel any inherent evil in this reptile lifeform. From my perspective, even humans and humanoids are children of The Creator, and I find beauty in you.

In order for your own survival to be insured, I urge you not to go off on tangents during these Change Times, engaging in science fiction scenarios.

Look realistically at who does the damage to the planet. Who fights wars?

Do not go shadow boxing at beings who reportedly look like me while Earth quite literally goes to hell. Your human inclination toward prejudice and hatred is what has gotten your race in this crisis. Do not take this prejudice into space. In fact, you cannot join the galactic community if you hold onto this. Learn to find beauty in all The Creator's life forms, learn to judge individuals, not races.

I AM Lita of the Space/Dimensional Intelligence, ending transmission.

To confirm Lita's message, we hear from *Celiera, a nature spirit of Earth* who is a regular telepathic source for us. Her conceptual name is "She Who Celebrates the River."

This is Celiera. I love you as I love the river, unconditionally.

I wish to warn you of disinformation being put forth by governments, sometimes through channels and other New Age sources, who are not "true to the vibration."

Allow me to explain: When humankind first emerged on the planet, he/she remembered the kindredship to Earth just as a child feels close to its mother. Deities and spirits were not perceived in embodied form but rather as energies. If they took the form of a crow, a lion, a human (or whatever), they did not stay in this solid form for long. They returned to being "of spirit."

The ancient Celts believed in the skill of "shape shifting" among advanced beings and this was indeed accurate.

In those days, each river had a unique spirit. Because humans respected and even worshipped this spirit, they took care of the river. Today, they pollute and contaminate the river, never do they dream that she still has a living spirit! A consciousness.

Gradually, humankind began giving his gods and goddesses stabilized human form, and then it became a contest to see how beautifully each god and goddess could be painted or sculpted. A god "had" to be in beautiful form, in terms of physical human beauty. The gods and goddesses became simply "super" men and women with lives which sounded like soap operas. Studies of ancient Greece and Rome attest to this. Human egotism entered the scene.

Now in the present time, there is much preoccupation on the part of UFO researchers and New Agers with various scenarios which seem to be emerging about UFO occupants. Some of these, it is claimed, come from newly declassified government files.

Disinformation Being Maliciously Dispersed

I warn you to be very wary of anyone who says he or she has "The Answer" regarding UFOs and related topics. There is much disinformation being purposely sent out. Humans tend to latch onto stereotypes, just as they did with their deities long ago, and thus limit or warp the human perception of reality.

If disinformation is accepted as truth, it closes many doors. It could even close the door to the human race evolving spiritually. If this door is closed, Doomsday follows. This is the saddest of all scenarios.

There are those who do not want any humans to know any aliens, ever. This is the door which is trying to be closed, for the selfish purposes of greedy individuals. They wish to keep their power and to have it grow. They will lose their power when the human race enters into cosmic citizenship, leaving the old, low frequency behind. Governments, militaries, churches, economic cartels, big corporations, all will lose their hold over the people.

Do Not Return To Darkness!

Humankind must resist the temptation to plunge back into the darkness of narrow, ignorant, prejudiced thinking. This serves only those few evil, greedy humans who hold power.

To enter into cosmic citizenship, humankind must give up trying to embody that which cannot be embodied, must stop trying to solidify that which is of the spirit. He must move out from under the shadow of blindly accepting stereotypical images and scenarios which cast "the good guys and the bad guys" so ignorantly and unfairly. There is more out there in the universe than "reptoids" and there is more visiting Earth than "little bad grey guys" who seem to have emerged from a bad science fiction film.

Please, please do not let this be the sum of human exploration into Space/Time. Do not let this be the total human perception of UFOs and their occupants.

We nature spirits have watched this happen before, when humankind's bright dawn was darkened by the insistence on superimposing human ego and form on The All That Is. The gods and goddesses became human looking and human acting. Magic was lost.

Balance was lost. This narrow, human-dominated version of reality, not only dooms humans, but all life on this planet.

There is one last chance to live, and I beg humanity not to throw it all away!

With abiding love,

I AM Celiera

So far, you can see that the telepathic thoughts and feelings of these alien entities are not at all frightening. Lita of the lizard race is angry, but justifiably so. Celiera is downright sad. But both have hope and both truly love Earth and even humans.

As I understand it, Lita is an individual who you would meet on a starship as a crewmember. Celiera is a co-worker of Lita's but as a nature spirit, she prefers to live in the other-dimensional forest world of Earth. There is great cooperation and communication between these two groups in The Change Times, and both are members of the broad group we call Space/Dimensional Intelligence.

Here is an extraterrestrial friend who wishes to send us a transmission which has an urgent survival message for us.

Hello, Diane. This is, "He Who Dances on Meteorites".

Goodness, that's a silly name in Earth terms, isn't it? My people have conceptual names, similar to the Native Americans.

Native Americans give names which indicate something about the individual, such as "She Who was Born on the Mountain." My name indicates that I am fond of "surfing" on shooting stars, as you call them.

I can read your mind and you are thinking of that scene in Dark Star where the captain of the starship surfs into the atmosphere, and dies in the process. And you are also thinking, "Who is this entity who is telling me unbelievable tales such as, he surfs on meteorites?"

I have not attempted the art of channeling before, so I did not realize I could read your thoughts as I send you my thoughts. Goodness, this is a two-way street, as they say.

Anyway, I do not physically surf, I do it spiritually. With my mind, in my mind. But it is the same thing as doing it physically for me because my race can experience events spiritually and it is as real as a physical experience. We can do this because we recognize completely and thoroughly, that the spiritual plane is as real as the physical plane. It is the way we *are.*

I Am A Pleiadean

I come from a planet in The Pleiades, as you call that constellation. A few years ago, a human channel received a telepathic message from a Pleiadean individual and suddenly we seemed to be "in." Everyone was encountering us and receiving messages from us. Our constellation was very popular. Then, someone said we beings from The Pleiades were not so nice after all and from there on, opinions of us went downhill. Both generalities (that we are good and that we are bad), show a lack of comprehension on humans' part. Let me explain:

Allow me to first give you an example: Alpha Centuri is the closest star to Sol, Earth's sun. If I stand on my home world, Sol and Alpha Centuri are part of a pattern in the sky which humans call a constellation.

What this pattern, this constellation, looks like, depends on which distant planet you are standing. Are you standing on my home planet or another planet several Light Years away? At any rate, Sol and Alpha Centuri are part of this constellation.

Now, would it be accurate for me to decide, on my far distant home world, that all beings from "Gee" are good ("Gee" is the name of the constellation Earth and Alpha Centuri are a part of)?

Then, several of my years later, would it be accurate for me to decide that all beings in the Constellation Gee are evil? Perhaps I decide this after my government launches a disinformation campaign concerning beings from this constellation.

Do you see the inaccuracy of this thinking? First, Terrans and Alpha Centurians are not at all the same race. Yet, you stand on Earth and look at the Constellation "Pleiades" and declare that all stars in this constellation have planets inhabited by the same race. The area of sky you call The Pleiades (because it forms a pattern from your perspective), is not composed of two planets, as our example of Sol and Alpha Centuri. Rather, it is composed of hundreds of stars. You cannot see them all with the naked eye but they are there. Many of these stars have planets; many of these planets have highly intelligent life. Are all races within this perimeter good? Are all evil?

To make matters more complex, there are layers of dimensions throughout the universe. On and near Earth, there is the daily (mundane) dimension and a myriad of other dimensions. There is the angelic dimension, the elemental dimension, the nature spirit dimension, and astral dimension, and many more. The list of layered dimensions is infinite, and that's just for Earth, and many of these overlap and interact.

Apply Logic and Reason

The mundane dimension is one of the most isolated, though of course you can travel to and from it, if you know how.

Consider the dimensions of Venus, for example. There is the mundane dimension of Venus which is unlivable with a poisonous, overheated atmosphere. Then there is the ethereal Venusian dimension. Multiply these by the many dimensions of each planet just within Sol's System. Remember to add the many dimensions of the worlds connected to Alpha Centuri. And this makes only the dimensions of worlds which surround two stars.

The area you call The Pleiades abounds with life on worlds which are linked to thousands of stars, and each world has many dimensional layers. Beings of these many dimensions can and do travel to Earth, either in "nuts and bolts" starships or through dimensional shortcuts. Some of us can travel with our minds and it is really like visiting physically.

Do you see how ridiculous it is to declare first that all Pleiadeans are good and wonderful, then to decide a few years later that all Pleideans are bad? This is the kind of narrow thinking which humanity must evolve beyond. All too often in the New Age, the same old human patterns emerge.

Perhaps the problem with The Pleiades arose because generalities were used too much in the first place. Stereotypes were applied to beings in a huge area of the sky which really have little in common; how much in common do Sol and Alpha Centuri really have?

I do not wish to belabor this subject, but the "New Age" does not mean applying the same old generalities and stereotypes to constellations instead of other human tribes. It would be just as ridiculous to say, "All Greeks are good. No, now I have decided that all Greeks are bad." However, you know better than to say this! But many New Agers do not know better than to indulge in this kind of narrow perception, using space-age terms. "He works for the greys." "Her contacts are with those Pleiadeans." "Oh, no, he is an Orion!" Certainly this is not what the risen frequency of feeling, thinking, and being is all about.

How To Tell if the Alien Is of Good Intent

Before I close, I wish to answer the question, "What if this being is fooling me, saying he is of good intent when he is not?" This is a very real concern for those who seek psychic contact with us, and this contact is very necessary if the human being is to survive Earth Changes and become a cosmic citizen.

Psychic research into your own beinghood, and much experience in matters spiritual, can fortify you against this kind of trick. Also, most enlightened people have a sharp basic intuition where these things are concerned. My advice is to look at the contact you have established with your heart and soul. Does it ring true? Then look at it in light of other psychic experience. Use your expertise.

Many individuals from Earth become frightened regarding metaphysics ("the occult"), and when this happens, events can run amok. There is that fear factor about which we have warned you, which opens you to negativism. Learn to sublimate your fear of the unknown, that "boogie man will get you," human syndrome. It has no place in your conscious mind as you seek psychic contact with higher beings.

Many of you have worked with psychic energies for years now. This may have included "just" an occasional psychic feeling or experience; it may have been experienced through religion (the power of prayer), or it may be that you have studied and experienced the spiritual/psychic world in depth and detail.

All of these help you prepare for these Change Times. But you know from whatever psychic experience you have had, that logic also plays a part. Logic serves you well in both the mundane dimension and the psychic world. It is never good to lose your head!

In conclusion, use your intuition, use your experience, and test the psychic contact to see if it is logical. If you have contacted a being, is this being logical in what he says? Or does he preach hate toward a particular group or person? Hate is illogical! Is the being you have contacted an egotist? This is not good! Does he or she give you free will? This is a must!

I have now given you my message regarding using your "acute perception" to discern bigotry from reality, and genuine positive contact from a psychic trickster. This channeling experience was quite enjoyable. Perhaps I can psychically say hello to some of your readers personally in the future. At least, next time you see a "shooting star," think of me!

In the light of goodness and the love of God,

I AM He Who Dances on Meteorites

We have not yet heard from the angelic realm, and now *Lea-lina* would like to communicate with you. She is an angel.

This is Lea-lina. I come to you in the pure light of enduring love.

Diane, you have not channeled many messages from my particular realm of existence and it is time we corrected this situation.

I realize that you do not have a natural inclination toward the angelic realm. You are a positive, good person but your natural affinities are nature and starships. This is as should be, just as some people prefer playing a guitar to dancing a polka.

Each enlightened person has a "base of operation." That is, each individual has a group of spiritual beings with whom he or she identifies most deeply. You came into close contact with nature and nature spirits as a child, and your adult channeling career began with the emphasis on space. Because you have a natural rebellion toward organized religion, you did not seek angelic contact. But now you realize we are not a part of organized dogma but that we are a real and natural realm which organized religion has used, often in a warped way.

Angels and Dinosaurs Come to Earth

I find it interesting that two of the most popular crazes on Earth right now are "angels" and "dinosaurs." Extraterrestrial friends with reptile roots can tell you that it is no coincidence that dinosaurs have captured the mass human consciousness and imagination at the present. Nor is it any coincidence, my child, that angels are doing the same!

We are making a huge effort to manifest in human consciousness and imagination as we truly are, not as we have been painted for years by organized religion. Our huge effort must be for this particular intersect point in Earth's history. This is essential.

We angels place special emphasis on the prophets who have guided Earth throughout The Ages, but we are not exclusively Christian. We find The Buddha, for instance, to be an inspiring master. However, we do always seek to glorify God and His Son, Jesus Christ. We also recognize that all souls are children of the Creator.

Though we know, love, and work with extraterrestrials, future humans, nature spirits, Gaia herself, spiritual masters, other dimensional entities, and other positive spiritual beings, we remain very much of Earth's ethereal plane. We are not extraterrestrials, and while we are natural entities, we perceive ourselves to be closer to Cosmic Energies than to Earth Energies.

When I say we know, love, and work with other positive beings, I should say that we do this while remaining almost entirely in our own realm. You will not find an angel running around a starship trying to fix the computer. But once a group of beings learns to contact other dimensions (which humans will do, shortly), the beings can work together in great harmony and balance. Space aliens know how to contact us, have done so for many years, and they are our friends. Inhabitants of various dimensions might be described as members of a neighborhood.

Miracles and Visions Perceived

When we do leave our dimension, we manifest on Earth to help human beings in what is often perceived as a miracle or a vision, such as those at Fatima. The Holy Mother is one of our strongest personas, and humans the world over respond to her. It is no coincidence that the Virgin Mary and the Mother Planet can both be called "The Holy Mother." On up the road, you will find these two persona become one!

As the Earth undergoes its Change Times, these dramatic miracles and visions will grow in number and intensity. Many humans will soon encounter angels and become fascinated with our realm and our way of being. The Holy Mother will manifest in a great number of places, to thousands of people.

As the Earth Changes roll along, our presence becomes reality. More angels are sighted, more interest is shown in angels, more people feel touched by an angel, protected by an angel. This will be a great comfort and help to enlighten people as they attempt to survive. We urge individuals to seek us out! I myself, Lea-lina, always welcome anyone who contacts me spiritually. Please do so. Close your eyes and you will "see" what I look like.

Humankind is about to step into the neighborhood of dimensions, leaving his own secure "house" behind which has so limited him. He thought he was alone, but he was so very wrong! Humankind had thought his house was the only dimension, but, "My Father's mansion has many rooms." And the universal neighborhood has many dimensions!

Humankind is taking this step because he can no longer remain stagnant spiritually. If humankind does remain stagnant, the race will die.

I urge any one reading this who wishes, to contact me through meditation and prayer.

In the radiant light of love,
I AM Lea-lina

An entity from the astral realm wishes to communicate with us now, assuring us that we will survive the coming Earth Changes, raise the frequency, and emerge into a delightful new world with all sorts of beings from various sources. She is one of these exotic beings.

Diane, this is Nebulise. I come to you in the gentle, loving light of the positive universe.

You have not heard from me before because I was asleep. That is a bit of a joke but somewhat accurate. I belong to the astral world, that reality which exists in the dream state.

The astral world sometimes has a bad name among humans because there is a belief that the astral world is full of misleading and negative beings. The epitome of this image is the incubus concept which claims a malevolent, sexual creature descends upon the sleeping person.

This is not what the majority of my world is about. Every world has a few bad individuals, just look at your mundane world with serial killers and unscrupulous power mongers!

Before I go further, I wish to state that I strive always to find the Christ Consciousness within myself, just as the great majority of astral beings do. We are positive entities, meaning no harm, and feeling much love and compassion for all life.

The Astral World Is My Homeland

When I refer to the astral world as my "source" I mean, this is my native homeland of reality. Your friend Amethysta, for instance, is from a source on a far alien planet. Tibus is from the source of Earth's shining new future. Celiera is from the mists of nature's domain. It may be confusing to mention my native homeland because I, like others, travel to a number of dimensions. It is only humanity which has yet to do this.

Tibus is a veteran traveler of outer space, and visits worlds such as the one Amethysta springs from. Celiera, a nature spirit, is known and loved on the starships. Amethysta, the big eyed alien, is equally known and loved by the forest folk of Earth. Therefore, does it surprise you, Diane, to hear that I am sometimes flesh and blood? Does this sound strange or frightening? Ah, but Diane, you sometimes travel to my astral world; however, you know it is not your native dimension. I am merely stating a similar truth for me. And I am also known and respected by space beings, future humans, nature folk, and so on.

Again I stress that it is only the mundane dimension which does not yet interact. The coming Earth Changes will change this too!

We astral beings are very concerned about the future of Earth and we are doing all we can to help the planet survive. It is our planet too!

Of course, if you really want to be confused, I can tell you that there are astral beings who visit Earth who come from far distant planets or from Time itself. But the point is, nearly all of us are devoting our strength and gifts to helping Earth survive.

Precognitive Visions Manifest

Have you ever had a dream about a flood which washes over your town? Have you ever had a half-asleep vision of a strange man who warns you not to park your car in your usual spot? There are an infinite number of variations, but these are examples of our efforts to visit you, to warn you, to help you survive. As The Change Times pick up speed, so will our visits to humans; we will give warnings and advice.

When various structured, money oriented religions came into dominance on Earth, they discouraged humans'interactions with other dimensions. Fairies and nature spirits were suddenly "bad." But, the worst thing that could happen was that you would have a vivid sexual dream wherein you interacted with an astral entity. Thus the incubus legends began and fear was instilled.

In fact, most beings from other dimensions are not as concerned with "sex" as humans are. Humans are overly concerned with it because religions have stifled their natural curiosity about it. We perceive it in a natural way.

Sexual Energies Mis-used

Once in a while, an astral being will use sexual energies to degrade or dominate a human being and this is disgraceful, just as it is disgraceful that alien scientists have done genetic experiments on humans. There is little which can be done by a human who is abducted by negative alien scientists but usually in the case of negative astral beings, the human has almost total control over what happens, whether the human realizes this or not. If you are having bad astral experiences, we urge you to contact positive astral entities because we can help you. Seek specialized help also from human psychics who are advanced spiritually.

The knowledge that there is a distinction between negative and positive entities in the "unknown" (including the astral realm), is a major step toward lifting the veil of fear and assuring a positive step into other dimensions. This is important for the entire race's leap forward which is coming up on the timeline.

Knowledge, wisdom, goodness, logic, and intelligence are excellent helpmates toward a positive astral experience. Get rid of fear!

The great majority of us would never take advantage of another lifeform and have no sexual intentions at all. The astral world and the dream state (a realm within the individual's own mind), are sexually active realities. We do not have a sterile world. But it is a beautiful and positive world for the most part; we do not have world wars, famines, or other mass evils which your world has experienced.

It was a great sadness when organized religions taught their members that our dimension is an evil place where no good person wanders. Oh, it was still considered alright to dream, mostly because they could not stop humans from dreaming. But the astral world, which is an extension of the dream world but which has form, substance and a complete validity within itself, was and still is, considered off limits and negative by definition.

Our dimension is very much intertwined with the waking dimension. Should lifeforms be wiped out of the waking dimension, our world would be very lonely indeed. This does not mean we would cease to exist, because we are a valid reality unto ourselves.

The Dreamworld Is Reality, Too

Many ancient cultures did realize our validity, and the Australian Aborigines still do; their dream world is their primary real world. Their waking mundane world is only a supportive reality for their dream dimension. We take joy in interacting with humans and other dreaming lifeforms.

We fear most an atomic explosion because this would rip apart our dimension also.

The natural disasters which are coming to your mundane world, we can help you through these. Listen for our warnings, perceive the visions and scenarios we send you. If we visit you, look for the true meaning of our message. Think symbolically. Consider that we have your world's welfare in our hearts and souls.

Often students of metaphysics wish to go astral traveling and to interact with us but cannot seem to accomplish this feat. The astral world is reached through dream pathways and there is a grey area where vivid dreams seem "almost" astral. Often, Diane, you have received letters wishing confirmation that a vivid experience was an astral one rather than "just" a dream. We urge you all to continue your attempts to reach our astral world without fear, because this skill is an important one for you and for your future.

The astral world often gives you the gifts of precognition and premonition. It gives you visions. It sharpens other psychic skills.

So, is a vivid dream always an astral experience? No. You must ultimately go by intuition, by what you feel in your heart and soul. But it is true that humans make astral travel seem much harder than need be. The conscious mind blocks many astral experiences. It does this for several reasons.

One is that the conscious mind is that part of the mind which listens to the rules which religions teach. I am not speaking here of the heart and soul of religion. I am speaking of the human-originated rules such as, "No interaction with the astral world."

Do Not Fear the Unknown

The conscious mind embraces fear and is the worried part of the human being which tries to protect the physical body from harm. It feels "the unknown" is automatically a danger and religion backs this up. Often it simply blocks out an experience which doesn't fit its definition of reality.

Second, the conscious mind wipes out astral experiences because it fears it will no longer dominate you. Every human being has this "split" mind and, therefore, a split purpose (animals do not). The conscious mind has the ability to wipe out experiences while the subconscious does not. The conscious mind madly wipes out that which would empower the subconscious. But the subconscious has no such veto power.

In the near future, humankind will no longer suffer this "split mind" dilemma, because the human mind will become whole. Spiritual evolution will allow the two halves of the mind to unite peacefully and the sum of the reality will be greater than the previous perceptions of the two halves. This is another way of looking at the coming risen frequency.

Future humans such as Tibus function on a whole mind/soul. There is no split in their perception of reality. This is the source of their increased spiritual and psychic powers.

You can see why it is important for enlightened people, then, to seek astral experience and to interact with astral beings. This, too, is the road to the future.

Of course, we would never force this; if someone is afraid, they should proceed very carefully. But most enlightened people know how to seek only the positive and how to protect themselves spiritually. The wonderful thing about my dimension is that we are a "bridge dimension." We are safe ground, you need not actually get aboard a space craft! We are accessible via the main highway of dreaming which is so necessary and healthy for all lifeforms.

Do I sound like a television commercial for the astral world? But we are so handy, and so willing to interact, to help in sharpening psychic skills to give premonitions and warnings. It's true that most of the time you "only" dream, or at least, this is what your conscious waking mind tells you. We are a bit more difficult to find than the dream world, like climbing a major hill instead of a small one. But the experienced soul has little trouble in returning, once the pathway is found and spiritual know-how becomes second nature. Much positive work can be done from our world, and you can join us. Many hands make light work!

Work On Achieving Astral Travel

Diane, I urge your readership to work on achieving astral travel. Do not let lack of memory convince you that you have not found us, trust your intuitive feelings.

Do you ever wake up with the answer to a problem which was bothering you for days? Do you ever wake up feeling extra rested and as if you had been on a great adventure? Do you ever wake up with preknowledge of a coming event?

In olden times, it was said that you had spent the night with the fairies if you woke up in these ways. Now, we can give you confirmation that you do journey to the astral realms!

Many star guardians use the astral world as a safe ground for contacting you. Together there, you can carry forth much good work. The more positive the astral and dream worlds' vibrations are, the more difficult it will be for the mundane dimension to remain so negative.

All thoughts, all feelings, all actions, all dreams, do make a difference!

Sweet dreams, and love to all,

I AM Nebulise

Micha, our extraterrestrial healer, has another message for us regarding our health in the days ahead:

Diane, this is Micha once again. Healing blessings to readers everywhere!

Is there an individual out there who does not have an herbal reference book? If there is, please be instructed to purchase one.

In the final years of the Twentieth Century, the medical field will fall into some disrepute with many scandals, several of them far-reaching and very serious.

I hasten to add that there are many good medical people out there who try their hardest, and that orthodox medicine can help. As we have said before, orthodox medicine and herbal/spiritual healing are best used as a combination with each other.

However, there will be events which do cause people to turn away from seeking help in the scientific medical field due to these specific scandals. There is also a lack of research in several specific fields, and this will be exposed. People may not want to turn to the medical profession when it comes to specific areas because these revelations will be shocking.

You are familiar with the quote from The Bible which says, "And God said, 'Behold I have given you every herb bearing seed which is upon the face of Earth, and every tree, in which is the fruit of a tree-yielding seed; to you it shall be for meat.'" (Genesis 1:29). All in all, The Bible refers to herbs more than 3,000 times, mentioning many by name. The Creator put herbs on the planet for your use, to help you!

However, how humans use herbs has been a matter of dispute or at least, hear say, because the field fell into disrepute in the mass human consciousness, at the time when organized religion began to dominate. Oddly enough, medical science and organized religion made strange bedfellows, neither allowing that Mother Earth's herbs and spiritual energies should be considered legitimate. There was no tolerance of herbalism, no encouragement of it. In many instances, the knowledge was forbidden and individuals were persecuted who knew the "secrets" of herbs. Herbs and witches seem somehow linked in human mass consciousness.

Herbalism Is Back

Therefore, as herbalism makes its comeback in an enlightened New Age, there is not a great expertise in the field. It is subject to trends and tangents. This does not mean there is no solid, real, and amazing help for you through herbs. There is! And there is solid, real, and amazing knowledge to be learned, wisdom to be gained.

Each of you is encouraged to gain this knowledge and wisdom for yourself. Do not rely on the latest fad or what someone else tells you. But, please, at this time, begin with an herbal encyclopedia, one which is reputable and tells of all the herbs which can help your physical body. Also, begin with a walk in nature, search out possible herbs. Get to know them!

If nothing else, I guarantee you a fascinating study. At most, you will gain knowledge which will help you personally through medical problems and through the Change Times when doctors and hospitals may no longer be there.

Blessing to all, and healing light,
Micha

I'd like to end this section we could have called "Meet the Aliens" as we began, with **The Tuatha De Danann**. As you remember, they are an ancient tribe who now live other-dimensionally.

We are The Tuatha De Danann. We come to you in the timelessness of love.

Diane, though you think of us as "Ireland-connected," we are in fact an other-dimensional race who inhabits much of Earth. Perhaps "inhabit" is the wrong term, because there are not thousands, millions, or billions of us as there are human beings. There are hundreds of us. We have kept our number in check out of consideration for Mother Earth because, even though we would be careful to take care of her, our sheer numbers would cause problems of waste disposal, food supply, energy resources, and so forth.

A more accurate concept would be that the domain of The Tuatha De Danann stretches across the planet. We are called by different names in different areas of the globe but we *are* The Tuatha De Danann. Have you ever wondered if the labyrinth of dormant volcano cones and tubes and the maze of inner faults within Earth, are large enough for a race to inhabit? Well, they are!

Have you ever wondered if there is any truth to the Inner Earth theories and to the ideas about traveling to the center of the Earth? Yes, there is truth to these, but humankind does not yet have an accurate picture of how it really is, any more than Star Trek gives a totally accurate picture about space voyaging. We do, however, have a vast network with the Earth, a world within a world. We are within the mountains, under the oceans, and within the land.

We Come From Inside the Earth

From this reality have come stories told by humans, of people who live underground, inside fairy mounds, under tree stumps, and in volcanoes.

You might be wondering why, if we are other dimensional, do we live inside the Earth? It might seem that other dimensional beings could mix with humans as "spirits" and never be seen. We do mingle, sometimes, sight unseen, but psychically sensitive human beings almost always sense our presence. You see, we are not "spirits" as such, not like your Aunt Betsy who passed away, is a spirit. We are solid, living beings, but we exist in an adjacent dimension now.

We are basically invisible in your reality unless we wish to be visible, which involves working ourselves into a special psychic state of mind. But, we cannot hide our presence forever when we are in your world. Usually we plan to encounter a lone individual when we do mingle there, but we cannot stay in your world for long. If we did stay there for a long period, it would take detailed preparation on our part.

As we have told you, we used to live in your dimension millennia ago, but we became totally disgusted with the greed and brutality of humankind and we turned "sideways to the sun." Our roots, we trace to the sky, just as legend says. For thousands of years, we have continued to study and to live in the mystical, spiritual way which was prevalent on Earth in ancient times. We chose to reject technology for the most part, and to live close to our mother, The Earth.

We have continued a close relationship with her nature spirits and a number of Earth entities for many years now. They are our beloved friends. Also, the Space/Dimensional Intelligence who work to save Earth in this crisis time, are our friends and co-workers. In fact, you might say, "We are them," in many instances.

We make journeys to Earth's beautiful surface when humans are not around, and our inner world is magnificent as well.

But we are not transmitting this message to simply tell you about ourselves and our world. Because volcano activity has increased greatly on Earth and will continue doing so, we must vacate many of our volcanic tubes and cones. Faults are also activating, and there is increased earthquake activity. These are not safe places for us to be anymore, either in the mundane dimension or in our home plane.

We have foreseen these crisis and created alternative homes and systems for ourselves, but in general, we are being forced out of our sanctuaries to some degree. We are not sure to what degree, the future is open.

The San Andreas Fault is an important part of a tunnel system which may soon buckle entirely. This is part of a network which stretches from the pyramids of Mexico to Mt. Shasta, California; then, of course, other systems take us even farther. We travel these "systems" faster than you could walk or run, but we do not use technology.

At any rate, an aspect of The Change Times involves human beings interacting with space and other-dimensional intelligence for the first time. That is, face to face meetings, handshakes, and working together as friends (that is, once the actual Change Point is past). In our case, this is not what we have chosen but what we will be driven to, when our safety net (Inner Earth), collapses beyond our being able to stay in it.

We Will Be Surfacing!

Tibus and others have told you that psychic powers are increasing for everyone; we are experiencing this too, as the Change Point approaches. Part of this prediction includes the fact that we will be "surfacing" more and more, and your psychic senses will get quite a work-out! Remember, we are both solid, living beings and other-dimensional by nature at this point. Once we were indeed of your world, which will be helpful to you in the current crisis. We can advise and empathize.

But, all is well as the human race takes the spiritual evolutionary leap forward, because we cannot stay hidden any longer anyway. Once we departed from humankind's side because it was impossible to live and work with this cruel, childish race. Now we know that it will soon be time to rejoin humankind as brothers and sisters, in equality. The human race will have grown up, following the completion of the raising of the frequency. We welcome him/her into our cosmic community!

There have been predictions by Tibus regarding increased psychic activity and increased encounters, and we know that many of you have written to

Diane to confirm this. These events have become and are becoming, reality. Many of you reading these words have experienced this increase, and have handled it beautifully; you have actually enjoyed the interactions with other dimensions and with "things psychic." This is most encouraging and commendable. This is as-should-be.

Now we can predict that you will be seeing more of us (The Family of Diane), specifically. You will also be given glimpses into our world, or what is left of it. Know that we are busy preparing to rejoin life on the surface, to some degree. Part of this preparation includes increased visits to your world, to meet human beings specifically. We hope to meet enlightened individuals first who will not hurt us, and whom we will not scare too badly. We are beautiful in your physical terms, but you will sense we are "different." We do want to frighten you with our difference.

We urge you to ponder on our Inner Earth domain and upon our vibration. You might want to imagine our world as you are going to sleep. It will be highly possible, then, that we can give you a better idea of it during your dream-sleep.

We are beings of God and of The Light, and we look forward to the day when the whole human race will be this also!

We ARE The Tuatha De Danann

CHAPTER ELEVEN: HOW YOUR PAST LIVES CAN HELP YOU

My first experience in being hypnotically regressed was when a medical hypnotist friend helped me look into one of my own past lives. That was back in 1979.

That look backward was full of synchronicities which echo in my life even today. I felt that I was a young man named John Locke who had deserted the British Army. I was able to give my hypnotist friend several obscure historical facts which proved to be true when we researched them later on. I had no conscious knowledge of British history; I did not know any of the facts consciously which I was able to give her under hypnosis.

I moved to Ireland in 1990, and I was immediately impressed with the dry stone walls which line the countryside. This was the first image I had gotten under hypnosis when I remembered being John Locke! When I underwent hypnosis in 1979, I had absolutely no interest in, nor knowledge of, Ireland or how it looks physically.

I picked up my mail in a very small town named Callan in County Kilkenny. I got my groceries in Callan, did all my errands in Callan. Of all the towns in the world, Callan, Ireland, became *my* town.

I sat down one day on a bench by the ruins of an old church in Callan to wait while my car was being fixed. I looked up at a building next door, and there was a plaque which said, "John Locke, Fenian patriot, was born in this building." (I should note here that neither my past life nor Callan's John Locke were the famous philosopher you read about in history books).

I was intensely interested in Ireland's Fenian movement, its hundreds of years of struggle to gain independence from Britain. And, here Callan's John Locke was a Fenian hero. However, "my" John Locke had enlisted in the British Army, which was used to keep the Irish oppressed; of course, "my" John Locke had also deserted the British Army, wishing he had never joined!

Another contradiction: "My" John Locke seemed to have lived his life in England. He was murdered by a drunken army jail warden as he (I) was awaiting trial for desertion.

Finding Past Life Meaning

So what is my point? Obviously I did not happen to find the place where the John Locke who was *me* had been born. My point is, as one searches into past lives, one finds the most amazing synchronicities! That's exactly what the first hypnotic image of dry stone standing walls was, because I then really lived among those same dry stone standing walls for almost six years in Ireland!

Also, the two John Lockes are a delightful synchronicity. John Locke was the first past life I perceived for myself, and another John Locke was the hero of a small town which will always be dear to my heart, Callan, in The Republic of Ireland. Of all the names in the world...

This is what you must do, my enlightened friend, as you delve into your past lives, into psychic contact with beings of light, and into the myriad of spiritual experiences which await you. Enjoy them. Look for synchronicities. Seek to learn and grow.

As you know, a synchronicity is no coincidence! It is an event which rings true in our heart and soul, an event which means something even if we are not sure what, at that precise moment.

With a synchronicity, two events are mysteriously, mystically connected. Perhaps we are not sure how. Two events are connected, perhaps, but we are not sure by whom. By God? By the fairies? By our own higher self?

We may never know, but we are left shaking our heads in delight, saying, "Well, there was something to that! Even if I'm not sure what it was!"

So it is with my two John Lockes. My life is full of synchronicities, and yours will be, too (if it isn't already); all you need to do is wake up psychically and spiritually. Take "the spirit" into consideration in your life. Do not follow the mundane world's example of only considering technology and materialism to be important. Stop to smell the roses, to look (or howl!) at the moon, to perceive yourself as a mystical, cosmic being.

This is Tibus. I come to you in love and light.

It is very important for enlightened people to consciously bring past life experience(s) into the present lifetime. In past lives, you gained experience which can and will be helpful to you in surviving The Change Times, then flourishing in a new, higher frequency.

People who treasure enlightenment do not just happen to become enlightened in one (present) lifetime. You have been working on enlightenment for many millennia now. Most of you have lived lifetimes on other worlds and in other dimensions, and these can be explored along with Earth lifetimes.

Your Lifetimes Are Simultaneous!

On the Home Side, we refer to "parallel aspects" rather than to "past lives" because this is more accurate. Lifetimes are lived simultaneously, not consecutively. It is as if each lifetime is a slice of pie; your whole self is the whole of the pie.

You are composed of the many experiences you are having in your parallel aspects. If you are confused regarding "simultaneous" and "consecutive," remember that time itself is simultaneous. Quantum physics tells us that time is not linear at all (not consecutive).

You should not be afraid to explore past lives because you as an enlightened person today, were almost definitely not a mass murderer or a wicked queen in a past life. People who had terrible past lives, are not yet enlightened people today. They are still struggling at a lower level of consciousness, hopefully having climbed a step or two, having learned something, but they are not yet seekers of enlightenment on a conscious basis. Sometimes enlightened people do have tragic past lives, but this is knowledge which is best to get into the open. Allow it to see daylight so as not to carry hurt or guilt around inside of you.

It is imperative for many of you that you explore several past lives because there is something waiting for you there, which will help you immeasurably today. It may be knowledge a skill you possess, such as healing. Or it may be a lesson-learned which you should be reminded of, consciously. Or, it may be a brave accomplishment which will give you spiritual confidence presently. Also, of course, sometimes a past life helps you understand a mixed-up relationship in the present with your mate or family.

Look at it like this: You wake up one morning. The moment is Now. You go off to experience the beach, not far away. You wake up the next morning, the moment is Now, and you are off to the supermarket. You wake up the next morning, the moment is Now, and you are off to visit a sick friend. This is how past lives exist, in the Now. Each is a new experience. But you are you!

Yes, you learn and grow, but essentially, the same soul who went to the beach, goes to visit a sick friend. You were not a nice guy the day you went to the beach, and Jack the Ripper the day you visited the sick friend. So do not have fear in exploring past lives.

Finding the Key to What Holds You Back

Your explorations will give you many answers about yourself which will help you in the present. Possibly a past life will give you the key to what is holding you back at present.

Looking into past lives is, in a sense, becoming a time traveler. I am a time traveler in a different way, but I also have explored my past lives. Just like yours, some of mine were lived on Earth, while other lifetimes were on a far distant world. Often your star guardian has shared past lives with you when he or she was in your physical dimension. The list of possibilities is endless. We are all on a grand adventure!

And if it doesn't always make perfect sense, like Diane's two "John

Lockes," then it is great fun to enjoy and learn from the synchronicities involved.

It is important to remember that you are you "Now." Do not make the mistake of trying to actually live as if you were in your past life. You have grown since then. Do not let it massage your ego, either. We have heard individuals say, "Well, I was King Arthur so I have to have a big house even today." Or, "I know a lot about magic because I was Morgan La Fay."

Consider for a moment how many people have lived throughout human history. Now consider how many of those have been famous enough to be known to us today. There are billions of human lifetimes lived, but only a few hundred very famous people.

Diane has had five people tell her directly that they were King Arthur, for example.

Now, it is true that an archetypical persona such as King Arthur, can impose itself on a number of sensitive, open souls. This is more than role playing, but similar. An individual can begin feeling echoes of King Arthur, will read about him, will feel Arthur's persona descend over him for a while. This is different than having been Arthur himself in a past life.

Ultimately, there is no use splitting hairs. If you feel the archetypical presence of a famous persona, so be it. We would not argue as to whether you literally were he or she in a past life unless your ego becomes overly involved. This can set you back on your pathway.

On the other hand, many enlightened people today have had much experience with the psychic world and mysticism in past lives. Remember that nine million European women were murdered by The Church for being witches. These were the wise individuals, the healers, the herbalists. These were the individuals to whom the people turned for advice and counseling.

Take Spiritual Power Into Your Own Hands

Spiritual power in individual hands threatened the conglomerate power of The Church. The people were supposed to turn to the priest for help, they were not to be taught to look into themselves for their own divine connection to the Creator. So, if you feel you may have been burned as a witch, you have more than nine million chances of remembering correctly.

Most people who will survive and flourish as enlightened individuals in the risen frequency, gained much psychic and spiritual knowledge in past lives. It takes a lot of experience and lessons-learned to become enlightened.

Diane has enjoyed doing many past life readings for her clients and friends. I, Tibus, channel information to her, but she also participates in "reading" an unfolding lifetime. Always we place the emphasis on emotions, on love, on human drama. There is always a past life which seems to be waiting to be told, a past life which the client must know "Now!"

Usually it makes perfect sense to the client as to why that particular past life has manifested. A synchronicity at the least, an amazing lesson at the most!

I urge you, if you are to survive the coming leap in spiritual evolution, to explore your past lives. You can remember them yourself, through hypnotic regression. Or you can ask a reputable psychic or channel to look into them for you. If someone else "reads" a past life for you, remember that you always have the final say-so, within your heart and soul, as to whether it is an accurate reading. And if you undergo regression, be sure you have a reputable hypnotist who knows what he or she is doing.

Look into your lifetimes on other worlds and in other dimensions, my friend. Do not forget these!

May the healing light of God and goodness surround you, always,

Tibus

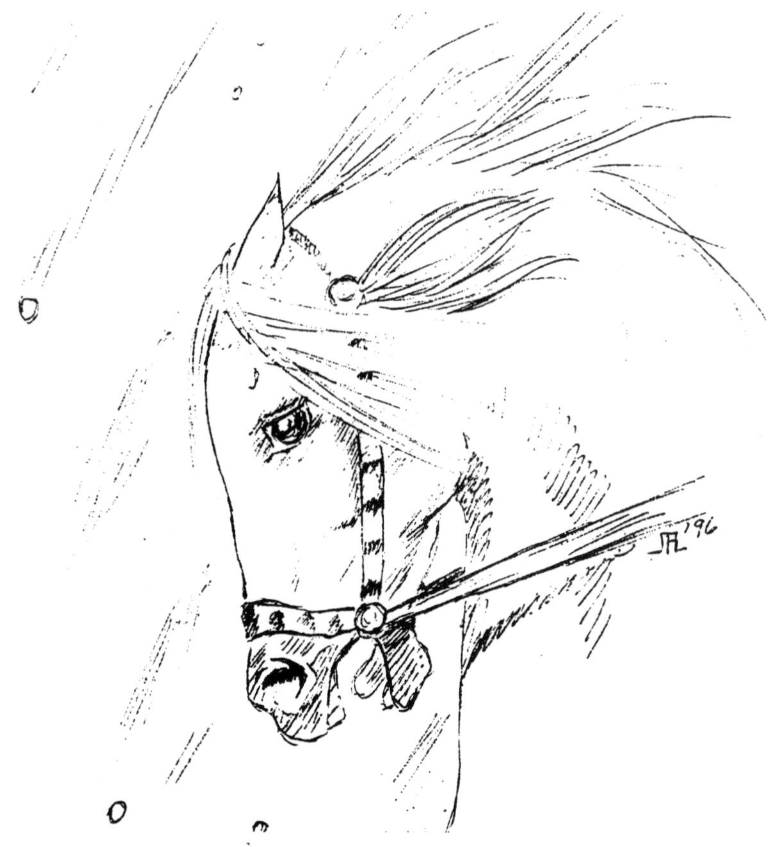

Artist Patricia A. Davey loves horses and unicorns. Is this an echo of her involvement with the mystical world in a past life?

CHAPTER TWELVE: LEY LINES AND BLACK STREAMS

As you become one with the Mother Planet, you must be aware of the concept of ley lines and a phenomenon called "black streams," which occurs in areas where there has been intense warfare or human suffering.

First, consider the concept of "ley lines." These are the psychic/emotional system of Gaia, the spirit of the planet. Where two or more ley lines come together, it is like an energy chakra in a human being.

You know that chakras in a human being are centered along a network which is similar to the nervous system but which is its own system, too. Medical science has not yet named this system, but it is essentially the psychic/emotional network of a human being.

As we said, the living being which is the planet has the same kind of system; it is composed of ley lines, and the intersect points of these ley lines. Where they intersect, there is much psychic energy. Often an intersect point is called a vortex.

The ancient tribes who were wise in mystical ways, built their temples, tombs, and astronomical observatories on ley lines and especially on the intersect points of several ley lines. Stonehenge and Newgrange are built on spots where three ley lines intersect. Many times, organized religion built churches on the spot where ancient temples stood, so that phenomena today in churches such as moving, bleeding, or crying statues, may be partially the result of the location of the church, on strong ley lines.

We also recognize that these phenomena are the result of the strong spiritual power of the religion and of the people's belief in that religion. Mother Mary appears often in churches, and she is a living angelic entity who is exceptionally active in her work with the human race.

UFOs Over Ley Lines

UFOs are often seen over ley lines and their intersect points. Also, strange paranormal events happen close to ley lines. This is indeed Mother Earth's psychic energy system which stretches all across the globe.

Often there are underground rivers which parallel or superimpose over ley lines, but ley lines are not "made" of water, they are pure psychic energy! Water is one of the four elements; these Earth elements have profound spiritual implications. Water in itself has great psychic powers. Consider the Native American sacred water places or the ancient Celts' holy wells which were taken over as sacred spots by The Church. The concept of "holy water" stemmed from the ancient knowledge about the healing power of special water.

Back to ley lines: What if a bloody war is fought on the surface, on top of a powerful ley line? What if ten years later, thousands of people are starving on that same piece of land? A famine has struck. One hundred years after that, the same two groups go to war again in the same area? Corpses cover the ground and there is much suffering.

In a case such as this, ley lines can become black streams of negative psychic energy, because they have absorbed the psychic/emotional energies of terrible events which have taken place on the surface over and over again.

Why is the Mideast troubled constantly by war and hostility? Why have the Serbs, the Croatians, and the Bosnians fought for hundreds if not thousands of years? Yes, there are political, religious, and tribal reasons for this. But remember, there are mystical, psychic, and spiritual reasons, too. Mundane reasons and psychic reasons work hand in hand, they are not in contradiction. The psychic causes the mundane, and the mundane causes the psychic.

Usually a black stream does not encompass as large an area as the Mideast or the former Yugoslavia. Often a negative wellspring is no longer than a mile of the countryside. In this mile, strange lights and ghosts are often seen. There have perhaps been several deaths in this area over the years. Occupants of houses in this area may have more than their share of troubles and bad luck. The rest of the ley line, as it stretches across the globe, is normal psychic energy.

Most ley lines provide psychic power which is positive. That is, the energy which emanates from the ley line can be easily used for the positive (the energy is neutral). But ley lines in some areas have been polluted by humankind's many wrongs and injustices, to other humans, to other lifeforms, and to the Mother Planet.

Purifying Black Streams

As an enlightened person who works with the Mother Planet, if you sense a black stream, you will want to work with it, trying to cleanse and purify it. Try to return it to "neutral."

As you send prayers and positive meditation energies for "Peace!" in the Mideast, Bosnia, and other world trouble spots, your efforts will be more effective if you keep in mind that you are working with a huge black stream area. Any country or area that has prolonged war and bloodshed, has many black stream ley lines under it. There is no way it has been avoided, and in fact, this is part of the reason that the trouble in these areas just keeps going.

Black streams are malevolent psychic energy; they work on the psychic receptors of individuals who live in such an area. It makes them want to hate, want to continue warfare. This becomes a vicious circle.

You will want to be sure that your special power place out in nature is not a black stream, nor anywhere near one.

Your special power place will probably be over a ley line, or perhaps at an intersect point. How will you know this? Because you will sense it when you choose your special place. It will be special because of its extra psychic energy, emanating from the ley line(s) below.

In the messages from the Tuatha De Danann, I got the distinct feeling that their dimension is intricately connected to ley lines. In the same way, fairies, elves, and sprites are more likely to manifest over ley lines. Such entities use this psychic energy, like the air they breathe!

As you struggle to survive and flourish in the coming Earth Changes, do not forget the concepts of ley lines and black streams. These are not just philosophical concepts. You will need to know how to work psychically with ley lines, to create a risen reality, and with black streams, so that they do not "sour the soup."

At the close of a transmission regarding ley lines and black streams, Tibus stated the following:

Can the human race attain Christ Consciousness? Can the human race act with love and compassion? Can the human race be as pure as Jesus, even for a moment?

I am always talking about the Reality Continuum for The Change Times. Will we have a gentle "1" or a not-so-bad "3" instead of a Doomsday "10?" Isn't this the same as saying that the human race must take responsibility for creating the next step up the ladder of spiritual evolution?

The human race must do this on its own just as every race in the cosmic community has done during its time of planetary crisis. We of the higher realms can help, can encourage, but ultimately the human race must raise the frequency on its own volition. We cannot take the step for you; teachers can help the child but they cannot learn the lesson for him.

Humankind Threatens Destruction

If humankind cannot take the next step in spiritual evolution, he will cease to exist. There is the added threat that he will take his planet with him, into lifeless oblivion. This would be an even greater tragedy, because the Mother Planet has such wonderful, diverse lifeforms. These lifeforms have done nothing to cause a threat to the life of their planet, only humankind has. And it is humankind who must save the day!

I have told you, Diane, about the malevolent influence of psychic black streams which exist in chronic political trouble spots around the world. These occur also where nature has been decimated. For instance, the Amazon where once great rain forests stood, now is crisscrossed with "black stream" ley lines, echoing the destruction of life above. These will cause more suffering to the Natives of the Amazon because nature will have seemed to turn against them entirely. "Bad luck" often has to do with a black stream beneath an individual's habitat.

I urge you and enlightened people everywhere to work on lessening these specific areas of negative psychic energy. Do not be lazy on this one or feel that you cannot help. And once you comprehend the premise, any psychically sensitive person can sense where a ley line has turned negative. Simply sending positive psychic energy to such an area can help more than you can imagine. These areas are very likely to respond to positive psychic input, because they are originally "of nature" and basically seek to be of neutral psychic energy again.

Do not let the snowball effect start. Once large catastrophes begin, we have a much bigger fight on our hands trying to stop the momentum and trying to save the planet. We must take each crisis, whether political or natural, and work with it spiritually to return it to a "1" on our continuum. In other words, create the reality where this crisis did not end the life as we know it, but was instead a minor hiccup in the reality base.

I send my love and respect to each of our spiritual warriors in these most difficult of times!

May the healing light of God and goodness surround you, always,

Tibus

CHAPTER THIRTEEN: NEGATIVE ALIEN AND EARTH GOVERNMENT COLLUSION

Throughout the years, our Space/Dimensional friends have sent a number of transmissions regarding the sad fact that negative aliens work with governments and their military forces, on Earth.

Our Star Network has been told about a disagreement which these two unscrupulous groups had, which nearly resulted in a war between them.

We have been told about the terrible mutilations of livestock for the purpose of obtaining genetic samples, and about the frightening abductions of human beings.

Our Space/Dimensional friends have protected many people from abductions, have interfered in the middle of other abductions and returned the human to safety, and have tried to stop abductions and mutilations entirely.

Incidentally, the negative aliens who work with the governments are relatively small in number. They are mavericks who are in no way sanctioned by positive extraterrestrials or dimensional beings. They are not from one race alone, they are not all grey or all small.

Space/Dimensional friends have tried to stop these aliens from giving technology to secret government groups; we can see by the leap in computer technology, for instance, that there has been in-put from technically advanced sources. We must add that nothing is "given" for free, the Earth governments have had to give much in return, often the freedom of their own citizens.

The good guys have managed to put a stop to much of the collusion, but not all of it. They cannot declare open warfare on the negative aliens nor, on Earth governments and militaries. This is against The Noninterference Directive and, besides, the positive beings of space/dimension are not war-like. They abandoned war millions of years ago. One can see how important the Noninterference Directive is, when one perceives how the negative aliens break this directive.

Leave Negative Aliens Behind

Throughout a number of transmissions, one point has always been stressed by our friends: There is really nothing one enlightened individual can do to stop the government/negative alien collusion. Instead, we must move on, beyond them! Their approach, their technology, their entire way of being must become extinct!

We must leave them behind and raise the frequency. Change the dimension, turn the page. The governments and the negative aliens are on the old page, our reality will be on the new page.

Tibus emphasizes that in his future time, the negative aliens are no longer in partnership with the greedy secret government groups. These groups no longer exist. Humankind has gone onward and such groups became obsolete long ago. In Tibus' future time, for a negative alien to attempt partnership with some secret human group would be like a man coming out of a cave with a club to kill dinner, and discovering he was in an elite modern restaurant. Killing has no place, least of all with a club. You just don't do that to get your dinner!

In the same way, on Tibus' Earth, you do not do genetic experiments. You do not make high tech weapons and controlling computers. You do not go into partnership with some secret group. This is absurd, unheard of. The way of thinking, doing, and being of the entire present reality will become extinct!

So, the only thing you as an individual can do to fight the government/alien collusion is to continue your work in bringing The Light! You cannot break into secret installations and demolish the laboratory. No way to get past those military security guards! And if you manage to do this, you'll be locked up for life if they let you live.

Do Not Become A Slave to Conspiracy Theories

Tibus has expressed some frustration at the many theories on government conspiracies and alien collusion which abound these days. He has stated that most of them have some basis in truth, but they never tell the individual what to do to stop them, or to avoid their dire consequences.

These scenarios can make an individual very uptight, worried, paranoid, and frustrated, but what to do about them? They send out negative energy to you, stopping you from centering to meditate. Or you become depressed and figure meditation does no good. They make you unhappy and restless. How can you carry forth your light work?

Don't you think that many of these government conspiracy and negative alien collusion scenarios are made public to do exactly that, to stop you from creating the positive new reality?

Who has the most to gain if the frequency is not raised?

Those who are now in power have the most to gain! That is, they do if they can keep complete Doomsday away, but they have their secure bunkers in case of radioactivity and other disasters, so they do not mind if there is widespread destruction. They figure they can get to safety. But they still want their seat of power; they do not want human beings to progress so that they do not need the overlords of power.

If the frequency is raised, human beings will not need their self-serving governments. They will not need military might. They will not need formal, structured churches, either. Individuals will learn to contact the Creator through their own God Spark within. Human beings will no longer be slaves to the money system once they evolve beyond it.

All this taken in consideration, Tibus advises you not to get stuck in the conspiracy theories and propaganda, or in the negative alien collusion scenario. Yes, some of it is true. But what can you as an individual do about it? Can you blow up the negative alien's spaceship?

Also, Tibus advises that often the conspiracy theories are only propaganda, spread by the very people about whom the theories speak. They want you to get off the track, to divert your powerful, good psychic energy. They want you to become depressed and to be scared, paranoid "sheep."

"All" you can do is to continue your work toward raising the spiritual frequency. This is the ultimate weapon against all the negative scenarios.

Here is a transmission from our friend with the large, wide eyes, and the gentle alien face, **Amethysta.**

This is Amethysta. I come to you in the purple ray of unconditional love and healing.

I would like to prepare you for the orchestrated effort which will be made by a new "team" from the industrial-military complex, who will attempt to "debunk" several well known UFO/alien encounters. We have already seen the fruits of their labors in the Roswell crashed saucer debunking effort which they undertook in 1994. "It was an exotic spy balloon headed for Russia..."

Roswell Autopsy

These particular efforts were offset by the Roswell "alien autopsy" footage shown widely on Earth television. This was no coincidence, because there are powers of goodness who want the truth to be known. They offset negative efforts with positive ones.

In the past, governments used several tried and true "debunkers" who regularly popped up on many television shows and wrote many articles and books. It was their job to "prove" there are, "No extraterrestrial visitors on Earth, no siree sir!"

However, the people's awareness grew and no one was listening to these professional debunkers. So, it was decided that a new approach must be taken. This new approach was to have dramatic announcements in order to catch the people's attention.

We have seen this "dramatic announcement" approach in the "new" Roswell explanation. Simple. Say it was a spy balloon, spying, of course, on the

U.S.S.R. That country was long gone as a political entity when the "spy balloon" was finally "admitted," 47 years later. Wasn't this a bit too long a silence to be plausible? One quote from this new debunking effort said that the material of the "spy balloon" couldn't be cut because it was "something like balsa wood soaked in something like Elmer's glue." I believe it was your P.T. Barnum who said, "There's a sucker born every minute." Apparently the military-industrial complex subscribes to this theory 100% in regard to the masses of people. We prefer the creator of Star Trek Gene Roddenberry's point of view which states, "The majority of Earth's people are Light Years ahead of their petty governments!"

UFOs Cannot Be Explained Away

We of extraterrestrial origin are watching with amusement this new debunking approach. In the future, other famous UFO encounters will be explained away with the same kind of "simple" explanation which "oddly" was not made public for many years. Also, they will have a "hoaxer" come clean after many years. This makes us wonder, "Can a hoaxer be a hoax?"

And, the Air Force will "admit" to testing a top secret machine, but do not expect to see this machine or receive any details on it, because this particular machine does not exist.

These attempts will give the impression that all events of high strangeness have, in fact, very down to Earth answers.

There is one thing wrong with this: These high strangeness events were not down to Earth! The explanations are carefully constructed lies, orchestrated and acted out in detail. This is all to shake the human race's belief in extraterrestrial life, and to demolish their faith in becoming cosmic citizens themselves by raising the frequency.

I stress that this new attempt is very insidious. Beware of it. If they can get people like you to stop believing in extraterrestrial intelligence, they have you and the millions like you, in the palm of their hand. This is exactly where they want you, and where the negative aliens want you.

The hardest thing in the universe to conquer is the human spirit!

We do not ask you to believe any and every UFO/alien account. But there are a some excellent cases which lead many of you to look further and become fascinated with the subject. This is what we hoped when we made your sightings and encounters possible. These are the cases which appeal to your spirit and to your sense of wonder and curiosity. It is these they will concentrate on, trying to debunk/disprove. They wish to break your spirit and they will leave no rock unturned to do so.

You always have free will, my friend. Your mind is free. Do not take what I say at face value, but examine each UFO/alien case. Make your own decisions. Look at the unusual events which happen in your own life. Use your own logic, intelligence, and intuition to judge. This is all we ask.

In light,

I AM Amethysta

Diane at the Harristown Dolmen in County Kilkenney, Ireland. This dolmen is over 6,000 years old.

CHAPTER FOURTEEN: ATLANTIS, LEMURIA, ANCIENT EGYPT, WHERE DO THEY FIT?

It seems to be a paradox that while individuals become obsessed with creating the future through psychic contact with aliens, sighting UFOs, and exploring other dimensional concepts, they often become obsessed also with one of the legendary civilizations of the ancient past, such as Atlantis, Lemuria, Egypt, Greece, Mu, Phoenicia, or Rome. There are other ancient civilizations, also, which call to people but these are the ones which beckon most often.

Of course, an historian would comment that we should separate mythology from reality, because Egypt, Greece, Phoenicia, and Rome, are documented as having really existed, while Atlantis, Lemuria, and Mu are mythological.

Our hearts and souls give us more information than our brains do on Atlantis, Lemuria, and Mu, because our hearts and souls insist that they were real civilizations. Many of us have very personal past life ties to them.

Even historians admit that a great percentage of human historical records have been lost throughout the ages, from pillaging invaders, the bonfires of censorship, the purges of power-hungry kings, natural disasters, and so forth.

It is possible that Atlantis, Lemuria, and Mu existed in that other-dimensional world in which the Tuatha De Danann still live; this mystical tribe has links to the ancient Celts, which is another civilization which calls to us. Perhaps Atlantis, Lemuria, and Mu were other-dimensional but Tibus and other guides have told me that they were civilizations in this dimension.

Apparently the records of their existence got destroyed over thousands of years, and only word-of-mouth kept their memory alive. This memory exists mainly among mystically inclined people such as The Gypsies of Eastern Europe, but many of them were murdered by Hitler and they have had more than their share of trouble in modern times. There just isn't much memory left of these magnificent civilizations, and what there is, is probably not accurate at this time. We must rely instead on our psychic hearts and souls to "Remember!"

Physical Evidence Destroyed

When you really think about it, if an entire island civilization is covered by a tidal wave, never to rise again from the ocean floor, not much documentable history can be left behind. Perhaps an occasional artifact floats up from the deep, and this has in fact happened. But thousands of years have passed, and the artifacts grow very scarce.

However, this doesn't explain why the distant past intrigues us, even obsesses us, just as UFOs and aliens do. Often at the same time someone becomes awakened to space/dimensional contact, they also become attracted to, for instance, Atlantis.

Obviously in one sense, "dimensional" opens the doors of Time itself. In the fabric of Space/Time, we are at one intersect point in the final years of the Twentieth Century, while Atlantis is at another intersect point on the fabric. Once we start perceiving reality in this way, we are not so far removed from Atlantis; one intersect point is just as close in our web of reality, as another. We can't (seemingly) travel back to the day before today (yesterday), nor can we travel back to Atlantis. Yesterday is just as far away as Atlantis is, on the Sea of Time.

But our intrigue with Atlantis (or other lost civilizations), is for a more specific reason than "just" the fact we have managed to open the doors of Time itself, as we grow in our enlightenment. Extraterrestrials and other-dimensional aliens were vital parts of society in Atlantis, Lemuria, and Mu, especially when these great civilizations were just being established. Rome, Egypt, Greece, and Phoenicia, and the Celt Lands, were heavily influenced by "people from the sky" but did not have the direct partnership that the earlier civilizations had with aliens.

Our friends of Space/Dimensional Intelligence can and do travel back and forth in time from these civilizations. They are not the "founding aliens" of these societies in every case, but they do have contact and influence in these places. Perhaps the same group of caring aliens is trying to help Atlantis survive its time of crisis just as they are trying to help us survive our time of crisis. Tibus says this is a bit too simplistic, but the loops and paradoxes of time travel are mind boggling.

Atlantis Is Still With Us

Atlantis is always associated with powerful crystals, psychic power used for better or worse, and with a water-oriented society which some feel connects to the beautiful dolphins of today. I have heard literally scores of psychic theories as to what happened to Atlantis, from a tidal wave washing over it, to a mighty crystal in the hands of evil ones, destroying the minds of the people.

Ultimately, Atlantis and other lost civilizations are best left to each of us to imagine and explore as we so wish. I know that in the readings I have done for hundreds of star people over the years, Atlantis figures in many of their pasts. It always seems as if it is more in their futures than their pasts, and maybe it is.

Some star guardians refer to Atlantis as their home source. Others refer to ancient Egypt as their spiritual source, and if this is the case, the star person almost always has an encompassing fascination with Egypt, too.

The biggest lesson here is that ancient civilizations have a message for us today, about not destroying ourselves. They have ancient psychic and spiritual knowledge to share with us in order to help us survive. They know what they did wrong, and they wish to guide us away from the same catastrophe.

They have all come and gone as civilizations, but the human race has kept going in some other form, until now. Now the entire race and the entire planet is threatened. It is no wonder that these powerful lost civilizations reach us in our mass subconsciousness (our ancient racial memory), and try to help!

George Van Tassel's Integetron still stands near Landers, California. This building was said to be a "human battery re-energizer". Giant Rock is nearby.

CHAPTER FIFTEEN: MORE INSIGHTS ON ALIENS

Hello, Diane. I am called the Lady of the Lake.

I am closely related to Celiera, The Spirit of the River.

You must have no fear of me even though I am a powerful entity. Like any natural entity, I can inflict damage when I am hurt or angry. With global warming, many storms these days are not natural; water levels rise in some lakes while others dry up before their time. Almost all of us are badly contaminated and polluted. Our lifeforms such as the fish, die.

Just like humans, we spirits of nature cannot hold in hurt or anger forever, and it is good for us to "let it out." I acknowledge that this might not be a good thing for a fisherman who is on the lake when the storm commences! In the past, storms were entirely natural, thus there were fewer storms. Those were in the days when we were healthy and pure.

I am personified in Arthurian Legend as a beautiful lady who dwells in the lake. Diane, you lived in Ireland for over five years and you were mesmerized by this ancient land and her waters; you know these Arthurian energies well on a personal basis. Merlin, otherwise known as Taliesin, and Morganna are your spiritual guides, too. You know that Morganna is not the evil witch which some stories portray her to be.

The Magic of Excalibur

It is I, The Lady of the Lake, who catches the magic sword Excalibur when it is hurled toward the lake waters. It is I who accompanies Arthur's death barge when it takes him to The Other World.

In your channeling, Diane, you have spoken of Excalibur being symbolic of the key to humankind's survival. The key is in the fact that an evolutionary step must be taken by the human race, a step which will introduce him/her to other dimensions. This step will also prove to him/her that the human race is not the only intelligent life in outer space. In this way, the magic sword will have been pulled out of the stone, and Camelot will be reborn. Camelot *is* a higher dimension, you know.

You have also spoken of Arthur's trip to The Other World as being symbolic of the promise of New Life; this promise is given by The Creator to every spark of consciousness in the universe, when the old physical vessel is worn out. Notice that I do not limit "the promise of New Life" to humans alone because every spark of consciousness, every lifeform, shares this promise given by the Creator of All.

The Arthurian Legend is a fascinating one for many enlightened people, including yourself. If you are greatly drawn to this subject, I can promise you that your soul has experienced life in Arthur's Camelot; you have lived at this intersect point in Space/Time. If this is true for you, I send you my special love and welcome you to your spiritual home. Ours is a powerful frequency.

Lakes the world over have long welcomed UFO occupants to establish safe bases in the depths of our waters. Did you know this? Just as you establish a relationship with a particular piece of land or body of water, our alien friends have established a friendship and linkage with many lake spirits as they live and work beneath our waters. This is but one example of how positive space aliens and Gaia connect to each other.

Alien Bases Inside Earth

We are more interconnected than you might ever dream. Positive space aliens have also set up bases inside mountains; mountains, of course, have formidable psychic spirits. In a sense, we might say that The Lady of the Lake and The Spirit of the Mountain are Gaia herself, personified in the physical manifestation of a lake or mountain. The aliens who have set up bases have gotten to know and communicate with us. At the same time, these beings have gotten to know the other-dimensional races who inhabit the mountains and lakes. This linkage, we all agree, is what is intended and what should be. There is love between us. We are One.

The negative aliens do not care about us any more than most humans do. We do not know them. They do not communicate with us, they do not respect us. It goes without saying that only a sensitive, decent, good soul can establish close links with such vastly different lifeforms.

You might wonder how UFO bases can be established under a lake, when a lake is very subject to being charted by humans. First, usually only a large, deep lake is chosen as "home" by UFO occupants, but even those can be explored by humans easier than the middle of the ocean floor. It is relatively easy for aliens with advanced technology to shield themselves from lake explorations. To be underwater is always a dizzying experience and "detours" are set up so that explorers go around the base without realizing it.

Incidentally, there are UFO bases under the oceans, but only a few space travelers wish to set up a base deep in those salt waters; there are a number of problems. Relatively shallow waters work better than extremely deep ocean trenches and valleys.

I remind Diane of one of her most spectacular UFO sightings over the relatively shallow Tampa Bay. Two brilliant white balls of light hung over The Bay for hours and one communicated with you telepathically, do you remember? (Yes).

I urge enlightened individuals to spend as much time as possible by a body of water. A lake. An ocean. A river. Even a small stream. Get to know the spirit of this water, because I promise you it has one, a living entity! You will be spiritually rewarded in one or more ways, I promise. If you need healing, this body of water may be able to help you once a close link is established.

I, The Lady of the Lake, will now end transmission, reminding all of you to take care of your Terran bodies of water. Do not pollute us. Respect us. Love us. Work to restore us to good health. This is for your survival's sake as well as ours.

I AM The Lady of the Lake

It is fascinating to me that the mystical "Mists of Avalon," otherwise known as The Days of King Arthur, connect very meaningfully and profoundly with today's UFO phenomenon and the coming risen frequency. I have a number of clients and friends who are drawn to this ancient vibration, as I am myself. This vibration has been one of my greatest teachers and I have learned immeasurably much from it.

Here is additional insight into the link between the Arthurian past and risen future, a channeling I received as a great honor from the legendary Taliesin, the last of the Druid seer-poets.

Diane, this is Taliesin. In legend, I am known as Merlin. I am a being who worships life, unconditional love, freedom and justice.

I was the last of the Druid priests, known as (future) seers and Bardic poets. The Druids were the shaman (priests and priestesses), of the Celt people. Throughout the years, we have gotten a bad name, our image being that of a dark cloaked figure standing over a cauldron, or some such. This is a false image, imposed on us by The Church in order to do away with the spiritual link which the people felt to us.

When I say "the last" of the seer-poets, I mean the last to hold onto the mysteries of the Old Ways which were in harmony with the Mother Planet, before organized Christianity drove the Old Ways into the shadows and the fires. That is, the bonfires of the millions of us who were burned at the stake or otherwise put to a tortured death.

The Last Holder of the Mysteries

I was the last holder of The Mysteries in their pure, powerful sense without the terrible memory and burden of what was to come.

"Seer" indicates that I am capable of precognitive insight and prophecy, just as you are capable of this. For instance, you know that something is about to happen on this planet, something of enormous importance.

"Poet" means much more to us than the concept of "poet" in the modern world. We believe that language is the physical vessel's means of expressing and celebrating the spirit. There are, of course, other means such as dancing, making music, art work, just to name a few. In fact, this celebration is, we believe, the best achievement an individual can make in a lifetime, to be a skilled and accurate celebrator of The Spirit.

And so, we hold poets in high esteem. Poets study many long years in our reality, using their basic gift, then honing it to near perfection.

In my poetry, I often use "I," such as, "I know the river. I know its boundaries. I know its voice. I know its sorrow."

I, Taliesin, do not use "I" in an egotistical sense, I use "I" in the Christ Consciousness sense. I AM.

As the persecution and prosecution of those of us who held onto the natural Old Ways began, we came to realize that The Church would not let us be, even though we were more than willing to let The Church be. We had no difficulty in encompassing Christ Consciousness into our belief system, but we noted with dismay that we were not allowed to co-exist in the world with them. The leaders stated that we must be eliminated because our natural, different ways represented "evil." We were a threat to their power, The Church leaders felt.

To this moment, we respect and incorporate the pure and good teachings of Christ. There should be no conflict between the two belief systems. They are One in the cosmic sense.

Paranormal Activity on the Rise

Now I wish to tell you and your friends, Diane, that there will be a great rise in paranormal activity in and near holy places, both those which Christianity took over, such as cathedrals, and those which have remained pagan, such as Stonehenge and Newgrange. This prediction also includes Native American, Hawaiian (Kahuna), and Australian Aborigine worship places. There will be renewed sightings of the Holy Mary and other saintly sightings in churches or on the outside of churches. There will be numerous apparitions, visions, and "energy forms" appearing, along with UFOs, in the final four years of the Twentieth Century.

You must realize, my friend, that you are becoming well acquainted with The Mysteries. Your research and explorations includes knowledge of Earth ley energies, precognitive insight into future earth changes, and cherished wisdom regarding life itself. It is up to you to help open dimensional windows so that The Light can at long last truly shine on Earth.

It is time for this! Dimensions will reemerge, reunite, and recreate a New World of Light, based on lessons well-learned.

Am I a "space brother" as well as a seer-poet of Old? Yes, in the sense that I work with The Space/Dimensional Intelligence. I am a co-worker of these positive and inspirational beings. Though I have lived lifetimes on far distant worlds, just as you probably have, I am a Terran by all definitions. I love Earth!

To survive the coming Change Times, you must also love Earth, unconditionally. No matter what happens to her, love her! Your love will see you, and her, through.

In The Light,
I AM Taliesin

An alien I hear from occasionally is named Alexander. I believe him to be a Future Human, like Tibus. I know that he works closely with Tibus and is the star guardian of a good friend of mine. He sends the following update regarding the mission of establishing "alien embassies" about which we were first told in 1990.

This is Alexander. I come to you in unconditional love.

I wish to begin by reminding you that unconditional love is the most magical of "stuff!" Do not place conditions on your love for another, but love, without qualification or specification. I realize this is difficult to do sometimes when dealing with mundane love affairs, marriages, and relationships. It would not be difficult if the other party would also love you unconditionally.

Another brief reminder: Realize that life is eternal, that each spark leaves The Creator's nest to go out and seek experience, then returns to The Creator, only to leave the nest again in a different form. Once this is realized, you also realize that "death" is not the disaster one feels it to be. It is natural to fear the unknown, to fear death, to fear the loss of the present physical form, but life begins anew for all of us, infinitely.

Now, to get "down to Earth," our alien embassies are in some cases, progressing well. However, we have had to give up maintaining ten of them across the planet, due to the threat to our staff and ourselves, from Earth authorities. We aliens are not at these places steadily but visit them fairly often, that is the concept behind them.

Eight Embassies Still Function

There are now eight which are still functioning but we are concerned about them also. The threat from authorities is not unexpected and we consider these places of love and light to be successful if they can exist on Earth in one spot, for even a few months. I would like to give you the locations of the eight now in existence, because our purpose in establishing them is to meet the people of Earth. But we would bring trouble down on ourselves and our friends who work at them if we gave specific locations. They must be discovered on a random basis.

I should add that usually we who look almost like 20th Century humans are the aliens who work with the embassies. The embassies are usually in bookstores, coffee houses, New Age centers, or similar small businesses. Once in a while, an embassy is in an individual's home. You might meet us in one of these places and come away with the feeling you have just met someone "quite different." Later on, you will have the certain knowledge that this person was indeed an alien. This is the first approach we have taken with the embassies. As the Earth Changes progress, we hope to be a bit less covert.

We have guided some enlightened people to our embassies, but there are not enough embassies to service most areas. This effort is still in its infancy.

Please do not forget our embassy project. It is exciting because we aliens are, for the first time, meeting human beings in an organized, no-surprise way. It is a start, and most necessary considering what is to come. We look forward to the day when we can welcome you fully into cosmic citizenship, my human brothers and sisters!

Unconditional love and peace,
I AM Alexander

Kell's Castle fortress was probably built in the 12th century. It stands in ruins today in County Kilkenney, Ireland. Diane explored its many crumbling towers and felt a past life connection there.

CHAPTER SIXTEEN: THE WORLDS OF SPIRITS AND SOULS

Very recently I have received two channelings from Tibus which shed some light on questions which I have long wondered and which I know other people have wondered, too. I want to share them with you now because we need as much advanced spiritual information as possible in order to adapt to cosmic citizenship when we make the leap out of this dimension. If we become traumatized or shocked in the very core of our being, we will not make it. To avoid this, we need the light of insight and knowledge about "things cosmic." There is no reason that human beings can't understand these concepts and rejoice in them!

This is Tibus. I come to you in love and light.

Regarding group souls: There are actually as many combinations of souls as there are stars in the skies. There are highly advanced, intelligent souls who are composed of many sparks (many souls), and these form one entity, one truly dynamic soul. "Group soul" isn't quite accurate because the individual components have blended long ago, and now there is really one soul. We will call this a "mass soul."

This kind of soul is difficult to explain because there are no similar beings on Earth. Do you remember "The Lights of Zetar" episode from the original <u>Star Trek</u>? The lights of Zetar were the soul of the planet Zetar which was no more. The lights traveled through space as twinkling energy. They had one motivation, one soul. They were all that Zetar had been, all the people's hopes, dreams, and potential, before Zetar's Doomsday.

A "mass soul" like this usually does not find a corporeal body in which to live a lifetime, not in the sense that we think of a soul living in a physical body.

A "mass soul" can be an influence on a human being, then move on as a sheet of energy, sparkling lights, an odd cloud. Otherwise, mass souls do not interact much with humans because humans cannot readily perceive or understand a mass soul. Once in a while, however, a human being is actually a component of one of these mass soul entities; usually this makes for a very difficult lifetime for the human being who seems very alien on Earth and who longs for completion.

Each component of a mass soul has individuality but the spiritual force of each is exactly the same, linked into the greater soul. Each component might have its own memories and experiences, but the identity and unique spiritual wavelength is that of the whole, the mass.

A mass soul can be formed under special circumstances, over the aeons, but also, a mass soul can be a natural phenomenon. The Creator has created mass souls just as He/She created individual souls.

Mass Minds Work As One

One step "down" from this concept would be the ants and bees of Earth who are physical individuals but who work for the whole (conglomerate) entity. Just as dogs and cats have individual souls, so do entire "tribes" of ants and bees. The tribe is the soul, so each individual is not a complete spiritual entity. In this way, the ant does not possess an individual soul; if one ant is killed, the soul lives on, unaffected.

The first type of mass soul of which I have spoken, does not necessarily find a physical body or bodies for itself in the way that people of Earth think of physical bodies. Usually they/it are happier as an energy mass, not restricted to one shape. This seems to most please such a soul.

However, the mass mind of a tribe of ants or bees, as well as many aliens, usually does manifest each component a physical body. Because of the oneness of this mass soul, the physical bodies are usually very much alike.

It has been commented that some aliens look alike and may be clones. There are a few groups who use cloning; they prefer to send clones on space expeditions which may prove dangerous. However, usually when humans see aliens who seem to look alike, it is simply that the human has encountered a "mass mind" race of aliens who are not clones. Such groups are linked telepathically and act as one. They might seem similar to highly intelligent ants in behavior because they usually don't show much emotion and they work very efficiently and scientifically. We have several such groups as members of Space/Dimensional Intelligence, and they are positive beings of The Light.

There are some such groups who are negative in motivation and polarity who are not members of our alliance.

Sometimes individuals who have frightening UFO encounters have indeed encountered a "mass mind" group of aliens, but these aliens are not necessarily of evil intent. Their alien vibrations can be traumatic for humans just to be around. For this reason, they should not be around humans at this stage.

Mass souls do not usually fall to the depths to which individual souls can fall. That is, one seldom finds a mass soul which approaches the evil of a Hitler, who was/is an individual soul. But on the other hand, mass souls do not often rise to the heights to which individual souls can rise. They do not often give their lives for others, do not achieve the radical creativity of individual artists. By nature, mass souls act for the good of all, because all is One.

Individual Souls Possess Courage

The individual soul will consider the needs of one individual instead of the needs of the many. Thus, a mother who logically should stay safe to care for her four remaining children, will risk her life to save one of her children left inside a burning building.

There is a school of thought in the galaxy which says the universe would be better off if all individual souls learned how to become part of a mass soul, then joined it. This would obviously be another huge evolutionary step, a total change for the human species. But not every possible evolutionary step is a good one.

This concept, if realized, would end racial and religious wars, because what Protestant would kill his Catholic brother if to kill him meant killing a part of his own soul?

Obviously there would be no "Protestant" and "Catholic" if the human race united as one soul. But there is beauty in diversity and individuality, too.

Some versions of the New Age tend to put forth this New Age Oneness concept. In Star Trek: The Motion Picture it was said that many humans had joined a mass consciousness which was "New Human." There are more details in the book which Gene Roddenberry wrote as a basis for the film. This joining was considered the only way to put an end to humankind's bad habit of killing itself (each other), for the stupidest of reasons such as race, religion, culture. Captain Kirk had remained a "dinosaur," an individualist.

This concept was dropped in subsequent Star Trek films because it is a difficult concept to explore. Unless you have "been there," or at least known souls who are part of a one-voice soul, it is impossible to imagine.

The Future Human Consciousness to which I, Tibus, belong, is not a one-voice (mass soul) consciousness such as portrayed in the Star Trek film. This has not happened within humanity; we have progressed and evolved while maintaining our individuality. We have "merely" used our decency and intelligence to overcome racial and religious prejudice. However, we have grown in oneness as a human race, a race which inhabits the third planet of Sol, and who proudly belongs to the cosmic community. As human beings, we have gained the respect and love of other beings in the galaxy.

There are many more kinds of souls out there, my friend. In fact, it is best not to label "types of souls" but look at each in its own right as a spark of The Creator's consciousness. For instance, there is a soul which is one life force but is composed of two physical individuals. These two succeed in uniting so thoroughly that they can reincarnate together at will. If they do not, they will feel incomplete their entire lifetime(s). This is a roundabout definition of "soulmates."

Defining Twin Flames and Soulmates

"Twin flames" are a variation on this: They are two souls cut out of the same cloth. They exist simultaneously, in different planes of existence. It is too simplistic to say that one of the twin flames is composed of matter, while the other is composed of anti-matter, but this idea does get across the "same cloth but different place/time of existence" concept. We feel that definitions which are too narrow have been placed on "soulmate" and "twin flame" in New Age circles. Each case is different and sometimes both concepts apply; other times, neither concept applies. Again, I would urge that each individual case be understood in its own right.

I can confirm that "one half" of a soulmate union will look endlessly for the other half and probably decide several times in mundane life that the soulmate has been found. There is always hurt, frustration, and loneliness if "the other" is not found. Of course, if "the other" is found, a union takes place which the Earth has seldom seen! That is, if the soulmate is in the same dimension in the present lifetime. The soulmate concept carries the ultimate commitment and also, perhaps, the ultimate fear of commitment. The universe can be a lonely place if the soulmate cannot be found, so is such an eternal commitment always romantic and positive?

Each enlightened individual should link telepathically with his or her star guardian and perceive whether this guardian is *the* soulmate. Some guardians are the soulmate while others are "only" a big brother or sister who knows and loves you.

Every soul has a spiritual family; members of your spiritual family may have a number of home sources. You may have an extraterrestrial star guardian, a spiritual "big sister" from the other-dimensional nature world of Earth, and a "big brother" who was once your loving father in this lifetime.

Also, is the star guardian part of a mass soul or an individual? You will need to take special care to get to know him or her if there is a mass soul involved; these can be very alien in vibration to a human being. If you have trouble in contacting your "special one," it may be that he or she is very alien in vibration, but this can be worked out once you know.

I have enjoyed sharing this information with you because it is something of which you will absolutely need to have knowledge, in the future. I send my abiding love.

May the healing light of God and goodness surround you, always,

Tibus

Artist Carol Rodriguez's rendition of cosmic "Twin Flames"

The question has come up many times as to whether the traditional Spirit World (those who have passed from the Earthly plane), is connected dimensionally with the worlds which our Space/Dimensional friends inhabit.

As an extension of this question, people might ask, "Does all this 'higher frequency' talk really mean that we are all going to die and go to the Spirit World? Is this what we are really talking about?"

Tibus answers:

This is Tibus. I come to you in love and light.

First, I wish to state that some spiritual teachers refer to the 4th, 5th, and 6th dimensions. This concept is a good one but we have chosen to go about explaining things in slightly different terms.

Diane remembers many years ago, being puzzled when talking to a well known New Age figure, who was receiving messages from a deceased loved one aboard a starship. This was in Diane's "nuts and bolts" days when she felt the answer to UFOs lay strictly in the scientific world. Since then she has grown wiser, realizing that this phenomenon of communicating and interacting with a myriad of other dimensions, is more enormous than she first imagined.

Some people go through their New Age pursuits believing that the contact of souls who have left the Earth plane is what alien contact is all about. But, the phenomenon is not limited to this.

Reading the Alien Aura

Often psychic readers of The Spiritualist tradition, who do a great job reading a message from a relative who has passed on, do a terrible job reading a space alien presence around an individual. They interpret it as satanic or evil in some way. The vibration is unknown to them, and therefore the "fear factor" enters the reading. Likewise, some space channels pick up aliens well but can't get a message from "Uncle Bob" who has passed on.

At any rate, it is my teaching that the 4th dimension is not hopelessly separate from the 5th, the 6th, and so on. I, Tibus, can travel Time and as such, I can reach back to when "Uncle Bob" was alive. Once you realize that Time is the 4th dimension, and that it can be traversed, all doors open!

We have access to Timelessness itself, and to any point in Space/Time. And I can confirm that some souls who leave the Earth as humans, do go onward to the higher realms.

Part of the enormity of the Change Times' implication is that humans will soon have access to countless other dimensions. Humans simply cannot be the race they are today, and handle this. They must evolve!

Most souls who pass on (from Earth), go on to New Life in one of the many dimensions which compose Earth. Some go on to other worlds. They literally go onward in Time to another intersect point somewhere/somewhen. I would have access to these dimensions as would anyone who has transcended the three dimensional Earth plane. However, the dimensional matrix which I call home, is probably not their home matrix.

I belong to the molecules of a particular intersect point which I call Home. My source. Their molecules belong to another particular dimension of Space/Time. If it is an advanced dimension to which they have gone, then we can work together.

Since it is hard to word such concepts, let me offer an analogy: It is like living in a particular house; we feel most "at home" at home, but we can visit each other's house. However, humans in the late Twentieth Century don't quite have this dimension-hopping ability yet and you must stay at home. But you soon will have this "visiting" ability!

You can see that your days of Earth Change are a lot more complicated than a climate change, a viral threat, or other physical challenges. Human beings have a lot of growing up to do, in a huge hurry. But I know that enlightened human beings will meet the challenge! I hope that my teaching and explanation helps you to some degree, my friend.

May the healing light of God and goodness surround you, always,

Tibus

CHAPTER SEVENTEEN: ONE STAR PERSON'S AWAKENING

This is Diane here. It is best I remind you of that, because this book is full of different, exotic voices, and the humble author may be forgotten!

I've known Tibus all my life, when I stop to consider the situation. As a young child, he was a loving presence whom I didn't question. Where did he come from? Who was he? These questions, I did not ask. Child-like, I simply accepted that he *was*. He is in my earliest memories.

During my childhood, I experienced the UFO encounters which I wrote about in **The Transformation** and these included meetings with Tibus. At these moments, he was no longer just a presence, he was a real individual. But child-like again, I didn't trouble myself about why this guiding presence had metamorphosized into a real man. I simply knew he *was*.

Also, the meetings aboard the starships were blocked from my conscious mind to a large degree, although not from my heart and soul's memory, but I am also convinced I had conscious memory of the meetings for a while after they happened. I feel the blocks went up for my own protection as I got older. At any rate, Tibus was here. Tibus was there. Tibus *was*.

By adolescent and teenage years, Tibus faded as I struggled with peer pressure, with trying to get along with the mundane world (this was before I gave up trying to get along with the mundane world), with trying to be attractive to the opposite sex, and so forth. Most star people do lose a bit of spirituality in the teen years, they are traumatic years for an alien in a human body. But, I wanted to keep the magic of childhood and I knew Tibus would be there for me, and was real.

However, my family and I had moved away from our Iowa farm, which was a place where I could be very close to nature, to a town in Florida. I had no access to my original spiritual source: Nature. There was homework, boys, not fitting in at school, and other family problems which added to my intense unhappiness during my teen years. This unhappiness kept me from close contact with Tibus. However, there were many times I turned to him for comfort and for help; then he was an oversoul for me, a promise of what would be and a memory of what had been. But the "now" was miserable.

I blossomed in early adulthood, finally figuring out I had a lot to offer the world even if I wasn't the center of attention in a bunch of giggling teenage girls. For several years, I probably was as unspiritual as I've been in my life, but I did enjoy life.

Tibus Returns To My Life

However, three years later, I became entranced with the "ancient astronaut" books, then moved on to other UFO and parapsychology books. It was then that I began to wonder if this presence/man whom I had known in childhood and who was with me even at that moment, might be an ancient astronaut, a psychic persona, or some combination of the two.

By that time, I was teaching second grade in St. Thomas, U.S. Virgin Islands, living with my parents and baby daughter Gianna. We had several amazing UFO sightings from our "gallery," which is what they call a porch in the Virgin Islands. I was inspired to get back in touch with nature. But this was a very different Gaia than the aspect of her I had known in Iowa. Tropical Gaia was just as beautiful and as spiritually activating, however.

With Gaia's reawakening in my life, Tibus' reawakening came too. Suddenly, he wasn't just "something in my head" to turn to if the world had insulted me. I began to wonder with fierce curiosity, who this guy was! I analyzed myself as to whether he was imaginary, but there was proof and logical indicators which said he was real. It didn't take long before Tibus activated himself into a more profound role in my life.

Psychic Excitement and UFO Activity

The next phase, back in St. Petersburg, Florida, saw a lot of paranormal activity and UFO sightings. Mothman flew over my head one night, my walls, lamps, and other electrical and battery appliances beeped merrily along at predictable times, with some unpredictable times thrown in to confuse me, and other crazy things happened. This was my time of conscious awakening.

For most star people who go through this phase, events become very exciting and active. It's important not to feel abandoned when this high-strangeness phase ends. I've gotten letters from people who seem to spend their lives waiting for big paranormal events to happen again. They feel angry and hurt when weird happenings and UFO sightings don't seem to come back. They don't realize that we do have a purpose here on Earth and once we are reawakened, it is time to get on with it! It is, in a sense, egotistical and selfish to just wait for the next big event to happen to and for, you.

During my awakening phase, Tibus was extra active, there were spectacular astral and visionary experiences with him. During this time, he became very vivid and defined to me in very personal ways. This period culminated with my hypnotic regression experience with Dr. R. Leo Sprinkle. Under hypnosis, I consciously remembered my childhood meetings with Tibus aboard a starship, which I detailed in **The Transformation.**

During this time, I also traveled the scientific path, becoming State Section Director for the Mutual UFO Network, and a field investigator with the Aerial Phenomenon Research Organization. When I wasn't busy teaching English as a Second Language at school, I investigated many intriguing UFO cases.

The Mysterious Laser Scar

I also attempted to gain insight on a laser scar I have under my nose. It has been documented as surgical (not a scar from an accident), by a plastic surgeon. My family has no idea where it came from, or when it came into my life. It has always been there as far as I know.

The high-strangeness phase of my star path ended when my daughter Gianna and I packed up our old Plymouth Valiant and moved to California with our Old English Sheepdog, eight cats, and assorted gerbils, guinea pigs, and hamsters. The "awakening" phase ended because I had gotten a better idea of what I was supposed to be doing in my life. There was no more need for the spectacular stuff, except once in a while. I let that phase go, I didn't hold onto it, waiting for the next "show" to start and feeling hurt when it didn't.

Our Guardian Angel, Tibus

Tibus himself was very much with us on the drive to California. Gianna was only 12 years old and I was the only driver. By the time we hit New Mexico, I just could not keep my eyes open. I have no recollection of the drive through New Mexico and Arizona, and I am certain that Tibus steered the car. I had his protection and incredible help again on two more recent traumatic moves. In one, my old car actually ran without water for hundreds of miles. It was truly a miracle!

Once in San Diego, California, in 1982, Tibus guided me carefully. At the time, it seemed we were having nothing but bad luck because I couldn't get a teaching job in California even though I was well qualified. Poverty forced me into risky situations and odd jobs, and I'm sure Tibus protected me. Somehow, Gianna, our animal friends and I, survived.

When I finally tried doing psychic readings, I had no confidence in my ability, but I could hear Tibus say, "Whew! She finally got the idea!" The in-person readings were a great success and I soon began doing what I really wanted to be doing: I began our **Star Network** in 1983, and I began channeling Tibus! I thank Timothy Green Beckley of Inner Light Publications for always believing in me and being my friend.

The minute I started on my right path, I had incredible good fortune. I also was able to buy a house in Poway, California, in October, 1983, having been totally broke six months earlier. Here I founded The Starlight Mystic Center. It was also here that I wrote my first book, **The Transformation**.

I know that I failed to get into teaching in California because I was not supposed to go back into it, even though I'd taught for eleven years. If I had gotten a demanding teaching job in California, I could not have devoted full time to our **Star Network**. And it has always demanded, and received, my full time.

So the seeming bad fortune of not being able to get into teaching, which I really should have been able to do, was actually good fortune! Tibus nudged me into a whole new field which I would not have had the nerve to try otherwise.

Star People Receive Nudges

Sometimes enlightened people receive nudges in their lives which seem like bad luck at the time, forcing them to change their jobs and their lives. But, you can change this bad luck to good fortune if you look to the spiritual path, perceive the larger picture, and listen to your guides. This is what the nudge was all about.

Since I began channeling Tibus to help others, his presence in my life has been always-active, always-conscious. He protected and guided me in my five year spirit quest in Ireland. My time in Ireland was an incredibly happy one for me personally. I loved the land with a passion I had not known since loving my childhood farm in Iowa. I photographed nature spirits and fairy globes; these photographs are truly astounding! I walked many long hours in the lush green fields and forests. I was Irish in the very ancient sense, and I had a number of absolutely beautiful spiritual experiences which I will treasure always. I know I learned a lifetime's worth of mystical knowledge and ancient wisdom in those five years I lived in virtual solitude in the mists of the Irish countryside.

When it was finally time to go, Tibus brought me to his starship one night and explained things. I loved Ireland so much, I never would have left otherwise. But today, I am grateful that I did.

I left Shannon Airport, Ireland, on May 4, 1995, and arrived at Kennedy Airport, New York, with my 15 cats, and 2 dogs. I could not leave them behind! Gianna met me with a U-Haul which we then drove across country. Neither of us had ever driven a truck before. Our animal family were remarkably well behaved, but our cross country trek was really a challenge.

Thanks to divine protection, Tibus' guidance, and a very dear friend, we were able to buy a house in the High Desert of the Mojave within two months. Here we live on 5 magical acres with several new additions to our family.

High Desert Vibrations

It is wonderful to be in the very spiritual High Desert, close to Giant Rock where George van Tassel started the modern era of UFO landings and New Age visions. This is a very special land, abounding in the Native American vibration, and almost everyone here has seen UFOs. We look forward to helping to reactivate this area; it is a prophesy that this area will be enriched with individuals of very high vibration, while those with lower vibrations are vacating the area. In the coming Earth Changes, we feel this area will be pivotal.

It is part of my Assignment: Earth to work with the San Andreas Fault which is nearby, just to the west of us. I communicate with Gaia, quelling her anger and hurt, working with the Spirit of the Faultline. I feel that I have helped to avert several huge earthquakes since I arrived, with the meditative help of my friends all over the world in our **Star Network**. I feel that we as individuals must work with our planetary mother on this intimate, personal basis at this point. It is for her survival, and ours!

To conclude my thoughts on Tibus' presence in my life: What has really amazed me is not so much that he is here, but that this guy actually has a plan which works. Sometimes I wonder if he just has good luck but I actually know that there is an astounding plan which we all drew up in another "where" and another "when."

Our Guardians' Plans For Us

Our guardians and guides do have a specific plan for us in order that we best follow our life's enlightened path. Being the enlightened soul you are, you would still have a spiritual path, as opposed to a strictly mundane path, if you did not follow your guides' nudges and plan. For instance, if I had gotten a teaching job when we moved to California, I would still be reading about UFOs and feeling a presence, but the optimum path would not have opened up for me as it has. I am extremely blessed because I am doing the thing in life which I can do best.

This guy Tibus does know what he is doing with his nudges and guidance, he does have a plan!

I have seen our **Star Network** grow, not only in quantity. The vibration of individuals who join us in our unified Cleansing/Healing Days is very high indeed. Together we absolutely know that we are helping individuals and the entire planet through these terrible days of change. We are doing this through our spiritual/psychic powers and through our close connection with Gaia, the spirit of the Mother Planet. God smiles on us, and we attempt to bring a smile and a higher frequency back to this world.

We understand the nature of reality, and how the enlightened human mind can affect changes on reality. Together we are engineering an alternate reality, creating a higher dimension!

The Joshua Tree (also known as the praying hands tree) has many mystical and healing powers. This one is in Joshua Tree National Park.

CHAPTER EIGHTEEN: ENTER, THE STAR PERSON!

This is Tibus. I come to you in love and light.

Up to this point, we have referred to you as an "enlightened person," but we know that some of you who are reading this are "star people" as well.

It is not up to us to say who is a star person and who is not. To be a star person, you have only to consciously recognize yourself as a star person!

Or, to look at it another way, unless you are a star person, the idea that you are a star person will not have entered your head. We do not need to identify you, because you identify yourself.

As you know, I interchange the terms "star person," "light worker," and "enlightened individual." The term "New Ager" is also applicable but we find a few inconsistencies in that term, and truly prefer "star person."

"Star person" indicates cosmic citizenship as opposed to being a citizen of mundane Earth. The star person is not chained to the concept of being of the mundane dimension. He/she knows there is more and he/she is anxious to be a part of the cosmic community. This is exactly what is needed to pull Earth through these days of crisis and change. Nothing more, nothing less!

The term "star person" indicates a seeking for spiritual truth and goodness, and for a better world.

The Spirit Quest Awaits

Many people begin their spirit quest in the middle or later years of their lives. Does this mean they are not true "star people" because such individuals would have been "seeking" from the first year of their life? No, not at all. Every star person goes through a reawakening process and this can happen earlier or later in a person's physical lifetime.

However, it is no coincidence or accident that you are on Earth at this time. Enlightened souls chose to be born on Earth at a particular moment so that they (you!) would be here to help Earth through The Change Times. You know, as a cosmic soul, that you have the spiritual ability to get yourself through this crisis as well. You have known this since you came to Earth in this incarnation.

Sometimes a "walk in" phenomenon occurs, wherein the original soul goes on to another realm and a higher soul begins to live in the physical body. Often this happens as the result of a near-fatal accident or illness. We recognize that the walk-in phenomenon is valid, though we look at it from the perspective that the accident or illness simply activated (reawakened) the star soul within. We don't wish to argue the fact, it is up to the individual it has happened to, to ultimately decide the exact nature of the phenomenon.

A few years ago, people felt that to be a star person, you had to have had a conscious UFO encounter or abduction, that you had to have a particular blood type, an odd backbone, low blood pressure, sinusitis, and so on. The idea was that your body was still somehow alien. This may be true of a few star people, but I do not agree with this premise.

The trait of sinus trouble has a bit of validity due to implants in some cases, and due to the nature of telepathy itself. These can cause irritation. Still, if you do not have sinusitis, you may certainly still consider yourself a star person.

We have always rejected the idea that you are somehow "less" if you don't have odd physical traits. The tag "star helper" was applied to those who didn't measure up with odd physical traits. We heartily reject the concept that some people are mere "helpers" while others are "real star people." For instance, if you cannot consciously remember a UFO encounter or if an encounter was not in the physical world, does this make you "just" a helper? Perhaps you are so enlightened that you did not need a physical encounter!

Being a star person is a spiritual reality, not a physical one. Most star people are very normal human beings. It was also said that most star people were born in 1946, 1947, or 1948. However, star people have been born throughout human history. A larger number have been born in the Twentieth Century in order to help the planet through The Change Times. We have star people in their late 80s, others in their early teens, and all ages in between.

No Place For Snobbery

I have always been opposed to labelling enlightened people (star people), into sub-categories. In her early years of exploring her cosmic roots, Diane ran into some very stupid snobbery within New Age circles. We are blessed that those attracted to our **Star Network** are, by nature, not snobs. They want to get on with the work at hand, which is to help save a world.

In fact, snobbery and bigotry in themselves display a very low vibration in the individual soul. It might be said that the true star person has no urge to label other individuals as this or that. In the same way, a true star person does not judge another individual who seems to have less psychic ability. No one should ever feel inferior because he or she has not had a lot of psychic experiences. Psychic ability is God's gift to everyone. Sometimes an individual who has had no psychic experiences can suddenly have an earthshaking one, when the time is right.

Each individual has some psychic ability; some lifetimes demand that this ability be used, others do not. Sometimes psychic ability can be active because of mental instability, so it may be that if you are extremely stable mentally, you do not have as many psychic experiences. I hasten to add that psychic ability is not directly connected to mental instability. In most cases, psychic people are very stable mentally. My point is, human beings come in all combinations and you must never label another individual as "less."

It may also be that at a crucial moment, a "less" psychic person will be greatly psychic. In the same way, a famous psychic might not have a clue at a crucial moment. There are no absolutes when dealing with the psychic realm.

Psychic Animals

Animals also have the psychic gift. There is not an enlightened individual alive who does not treasure the Creator's Animal and Plant Kingdoms. Love and protect as many animal friends as you can. Save as many trees as you can, because they are living, feeling, conscious beings. To nurture other lifeforms, this is the star way. Be empathetic, to all life!

May I repeat an important point? An enlightened person has chosen to live at this point in Earth's history. Star people are now involved in ecological projects and efforts to help animals; others help feed homeless people or assist the elderly.

However, a number of star people are handicapped in some way, through old age, an adverse living situation, or physical ailment. Do not despair because you can still help to save yourself and Earth - through psychic/spiritual pathways!

We treasure our **Star Network** because it is a telepathic network, not dependent on physical actions.

The reason enlightened souls are on Earth at this time is to change it through psychic methods. You are not here to literally move mounds of sand to stop a tidal wave, you are here to spiritually influence the frequency, thus quelling Earth's anger. You are not here to physically build tall new buildings, you are here to psychically create a new reality, to telepathically engineer a better dimension.

If you can also help physically in these Earth Changes, then that is a blessing indeed!

It is my dream that every human will one day become an enlightened star person. I know, however, that this is unrealistic. But when the frequency is raised, those human beings who can spiritually take the step upward, can and will achieve cosmic citizenship. Those who cannot achieve this step, will die. But years before this, individuals like you will have paved the way for the survival of some of the human race; you will have made a path for those who were capable of evolving spiritually.

May the healing light of God and goodness surround you, always,
Tibus

CHAPTER NINETEEN: GETTING READY FOR MEDITATION WHICH WORKS

Centering is a precious skill which helps in your every day life, moment to moment, as well as during meditation. It is a difficult term to define, but we feel this comes closest: When you feel the loving glow of your own heart and soul, you are centered.

A nature spirit once told me, "My friend, you should be very proud of the fact you are eccentric and march to a different drummer. Be proud you are not comfortable in the artificial, human made world. Have you ever been shamed of your difference? Yes, you have, in the days when you were not so wise. At this point in time, you must use your specialness beyond all bounds of what you might imagine possible, and give what you are best at giving: Love. We nature spirits seek your love, and so do the trees, the animals, the birds, the plants. Gaia herself seeks your love, which gives her badly needed healing. Your love will be just that iota of love which will see her through this crisis. It is very important that you keep yourself centered these days."

So before formal meditation, get yourself centered. Spending a few moments out in nature does wonders for me, always re-establishing my own center. Put your mundane problems out of your head for a few moments; meditation will help you get on top of them, too, so you are not neglecting them.

Overcoming Mundane Static

Our <u>Star Network</u> refers to "mundane static" when speaking of all the daily hassles and problems which try to keep you from establishing serenity and centering for meditation, and for building up your psychic power. The biggest enemy to your own meditative and psychic power is mundane static. It can make concentration very difficult, or it can even interfere with your finding a period of time when you can meditate. Mundane static can keep you running in circles, bad situations getting worse. Centering and serenity is mandatory, even in digging out of mundane holes, let alone for enlightened meditation!

So, take some deep breaths, talk to one of your animal friends, work with one of your favorite plants, take a short walk outside, or just close your eyes and rub your forehead, but establish your center! Feel the warm vibration of your own being!

As Carlos Castenada said, "Turn off the internal dialogue."

Let's think for a moment about how you as a spark of consciousness, reestablish the dimension you live in, each day. You get out of bed thinking, "Where are my shoes? Let me turn on that light. I'll eat my breakfast, then I'll start the car. Oh, the tree outside is nice and green." Each morning, you recreate the dimension in which you live. You reaffirm the details of your daily reality. You enforce a closure on your world.

If you can stop this internal dialogue when you are walking in nature, meditating, or just being quiet, you will find that this narrow reality begins to melt away, and other realms can be perceived. Meditation becomes much more powerful.

It is a blessing if you are a serene, well centered person by nature, as many enlightened people are, then your internal dialogue is quiet sometimes, anyway.

In Balance Lies Magic

Always seek balance, because in balance lies all psychic power. To be in perfect alignment with the cosmos, is to find real power.

What is meditation? That is a good question, because it is a word which is widely used in the New Age, but which seldom is explained. Do not feel bad if you are not an expert on it, because no one is. Even those who are very experienced at meditation and psychic contact with other realms, find that the degree of their success varies from one effort to another.

Part of the problem lies in the inadequacy of the language system rather than the failure of achieving the desired frame of mind and spirit. Language does not reflect what has not yet been experienced by the human race as a whole. Since you as an enlightened person are blazing new spiritual trails, you might consider that the language is lagging behind you. There does not seem to be a word which reflects the opening of spiritual channels.

The daily world tends to teach us that "meditation" means something similar to praying, only without formal religious focus. We are taught that "to meditate" means to send something "outward," with effort.

Meditation can mean this, but it doesn't have to. This kind of meditating usually only takes place after spiritual channels have been opened. This "tangibly sending outward" is a specialized form of meditation.

When you take a long walk, you usually find your spiritual channels opening. When you take a long ride on a train, plane, or bus, you might find your spiritual channels opening because your hands and feet have to be still, and your mind is not around household or business worries. This is also meditating; it is the basis for more specialized forms of meditation. This is all you need to be doing, in most cases.

Be Natural, Center Yourself

Then, let the energy flow naturally. Simply come into a state of "positive receiving." Don't make meditating too difficult an exercise; in fact, it should be quite the opposite, like a cool drink of spiritual water on a hot day in the mundane world!

Wash yourself with goodness each time before you meditate. To do this, you need to find a symbol for goodness which is meaningful to your soul. I wash myself in golden/white light, and this is my symbol for expressing the good and Godly intent of my meditation and my seeking of contact. I call it "golden/white light" because I see this light in a particular way in my mind's eye. It has an aura to it which blends soft gold with brilliant white streaks of light, almost like blending two kinds of cake batter together slightly.

Even if I just take a walk out in nature and open my spiritual channels, I take a deep breath before the walk and creatively visualize the golden/white light of my good intent. I perceive it washing over me, like a fresh waterfall, invigorating and rejuvenating.

You may want to find another symbol of your good intent, such as verbally reaffirming the existence of God, or reaffirming your aspiration to Christ Consciousness. Or, you may have a special gemstone or other natural object which symbolizes that you are of good intent. If you pick up this gemstone and hold it a few moments, you reaffirm your intentions. Or, if you wish to literally wash yourself, applying a few drops of special water, this also confirms your good intent.

This exercise is important because it gives you protection from negative energies and entities. Contacting negatives is truly not a huge problem if your basic intent is good, even without formal protection. If someone meditates on destroying another person, negatives will be attracted to his or her energies like a magnet. Hatred, jealousy, envy, greed, all attract negatives. But if you are working on healing/helping yourself, another person or lifeform, or the planet, negative energies will find you boring.

Be of Good Intent

Actually, the negative energies will be in a completely different universe and not be anywhere near you in the first place. When you meditate with good intent, you are safer from negative energies and entities than you are going about household or business chores. This is because your good intent is at the far end of the spectrum away from having bad intent, not in the middle of the emotional spectrum. But because you do open spiritual channels when you meditate, it is best to formally wash yourself in good intent.

In the spiritual realm which has everything to do with "consciousness," this declaration from your consciousness of its basic good intent offers complete safety from negatives. Remember to keep a feeling of fear away from your meditation time. Fear can be a real wildcard in meditative and contact efforts and there is no need to feel this, because you absolutely know that you will contact only beings of God and goodness.

We hope that every reader of this book will join us in a Cleansing/Healing Day. Our **Star Network** has one of these united spiritual efforts to save the planet at least once a month.

Sometimes Tibus designates a Cleansing/Healing Day which is to benefit our own personal health rather than to primarily heal the planet. Our star guardians always join the rest of us psychically, adding their considerable psychic power. Those of us who have specific ailments receive help. Others receive renewed strength and energy. It is very easy to run low on energy in these Change Times because the mundane dimension is unraveling and things fall apart very easily in all walks of life. Meanwhile, enlightened people become more alien in the mundane dimension, and this is difficult also.

Join Us For Special Meditation

There are also special Cleansing/Healing Days when our individual star guardians and spirit guides attempt to contact us and make their role in our lives more active.

The dates for our Cleansing/Healing Days are given each month in **The Star Network Heartline** and in our four-issues-a-year publication, **The Change Times Quarterly**.

The Heartline has been going since May, 1983, and has served star people and enlightened people across the globe without fail. I have proudly never missed putting out an issue, even during several of my traumatic overseas moves. Most of my subscribers have been with me for years and are my good friends. They tell me that **The Heartline** is their trusted friend and has helped them out of depression and confusion; they say it has been a guiding light for them. I urge the readers of this book to give **The Star Network Heartline** a try. I will send you a sample **Heartline** if you write to me.

The Quarterly began in 1990 and has also arrived at doorsteps, without fail. I am proud that the predictions and warnings given in it have proven to be accurate most of the time.

Should We Use Crystals?

Finally, I wish to address the question of whether you should use meditative helpmates such as gemstones, crystals, or other natural objects.

I say "natural objects" because I cannot perceive using an object as a helpmate which is not made by nature. It seems to me that if you use an object to assist you, it must be natural.

I have had lovely meditative and contact experiences using natural objects such as feathers, nuts, leaves, and even twigs.

You can use stones from your back yard, too. So, you do not need to buy expensive crystals.

However, many people do find that crystals and gemstones are extremely helpful, and they do have very dynamic energies. Native Americans feel that any object has an essence, almost like a soul. Certainly gemstones and crystals have this living essence which can blend with your unique essence, enhancing your vibration.

Of the many friends I have made through our **Star Network** some feel natural objects, especially crystals and gemstones, are extremely helpful to them and they almost always use them in meditation and contact. Others feel that objects don't help, and they usually do not use them. In short, it is up to you! Try it both ways and see what is right for you.

If you do use natural objects, you will want to choose special ones which work for you and which compliment your energies. Find the crystal which works for you, not necessarily the crystal which is showiest.

Try different gemstones to see which suits you. It might be that rose quartz is just right for you whereas citrine is not. The vibration of lapis lazuli might be great for you and even help heal a medical problem, but carnelian might rub your energies the wrong way. And remember that you want to find just the right lapis (or whatever gemstone), not just any lapis for your special meditative helpmate. Some people have just one gemstone they always use while others have many meditative helpmates.

The meditations we are about to give you, do include natural objects as helpmates, to boost your energies. But you are welcome to use the basic meditation without a helpmate if you wish. It is up to you!

CHAPTER TWENTY: MEDITATIONS FOR THESE CHANGE TIMES

A powerful meditation to be used with White Quartz, with a foreword from Tibus

This is Tibus. I come to you in love and light.

Our clients and friends have given us feedback on the "hands on" meditations we have given from time to time, using natural objects such as crystals, gemstones, natural pieces of quartz, feathers, leaves, flowers, rocks, wood pieces and similar objects. Often we have instructed our friends to place these objects in a circle or a particular design, and then run their hand over the pattern in a particular way. Apparently these meditations *work* and we agree from our personal experience. We on the Home Side also meditate, and I am about to give you several of our most effective meditations.

I feel these "hands on" meditations work remarkably well partially because they involve your whole self. When you meditate with the mind only, the hands fidget, or want to, and the physical realm tries to reestablish itself. Have you ever had your nose itch or your stomach rumble during meditation? It tends to "blow it" for a few minutes, at least.

Of course, meditation is entirely in your head, so to speak, but we are physical creatures of the dimension in which we find ourselves; so for many people, it is helpful to involve the whole self.

Use Natural Objects So Gaia Will Know

Meditations using natural objects are effective for a much deeper reason also: They allow Gaia, the spirit of the Mother Planet, to know that you are using her natural creations to communicate with her. The ancient people did this who had mystical knowledge; in fact, they used huge natural objects like standing stones. Natural objects are a vital key to communicating with the Mother Planet and her brother, The Cosmos.

They are also most helpful in communicating with higher beings in other realms. These natural objects become virtual teleports which exist in both dimensions, yours, and that of the being with whom you wish to communicate. They help higher beings and Mother Earth herself know you are seeking contact. The ancient wise people knew this, as do we of Space/Dimensional Intelligence.

Modern humanity lost this concept along the way. Would the careful arrangement of leaves in a counterclockwise direction mean anything to a business tycoon? No. But they meant something to the ancient wise people before the Earth got ruined by human made evils. They mean something to star guardians as well.

The Haunted State Quarry

When Diane was in Ireland, I guided her to an abandoned slate quarry near Windgap, in County Kilkenny. Diane soon discovered that behind the quarry, archeologists were escavating a Druid temple and stellar observatory which is over 6,000 years old. It is decorated with sparkling white quartz. This is a beautiful but haunted area, as those of you know, who have seen Diane's video, Diane's Magical Mystery Tour of Ireland. Here she gathered some very special Irish White Quartz which readers of **The Star Network Heartline** shared. I have recently guided her to a hill of pure White Quartz right next to Giant Rock, which was the sight of UFO landings and contactee conferences back in the 1950s. Both the Irish white quartz and the Giant Rock High Desert white quartz are very powerful!

White quartz can be found in many areas and if you wish to use a piece from your own backyard, that is fine, too. Or, if you wish to do these meditations with another natural object other than white quartz, that is your choice.

White quartz is used very effectively for healing as well as communication with higher dimensions. Use your white quartz always with love and good intent. Use it to bring The Light! It is not elaborate, it is very simple, but it is among the most powerful stones you can use psychically. It is pure spiritual power and we urge you to give it a try.

Get to know an individual piece of it as your friend. Hold it for a while. Feel it warming. Blend your vibrations and your molecules with those of the white quartz. Do this before meditation and energies will be more dynamic.

Most people prefer one hand or the other as their "psychic hand." Your psychic hand may be the opposite of the hand which does everyday work. At any rate, see which hand seems to have the most open conduit of mystical energy. Which hand is most connected to your inner spirit?

White Quartz Meditation

Place your white quartz in front of you. Take three deep breaths. Relax. Relax neck muscles, relax back muscles. Relax every inch of you, down to your toes. Take another deep breath. Now creatively visualize your mind, heart, and soul, washed in the golden/white light of goodness and God-ness.

Pick up your white quartz in your hand. Blend your molecules with that of the quartz. Know its ripples, ridges, edges, and shape. Feel it grow warmer in your hand, becoming energized to your vibrations.

Now close your eyes, with your head tipped slightly upward. Still holding your white quartz, feel the energies swirling and warming within it. Feel the energies of the higher realms washing through your mind, heart, and soul. Now see what comes. Feel what comes...

Images. Thoughts. Sensitivities. Insights. Simple serenity. centering. balance. See what comes...

Now, reach out, direct your powerful and good energies toward your own star guardian. This being of love and light watches over you. Protects you. Guides you. The star guardian is closer than you realize to you. It is easy to connect with the star guardian; you realize that his (her) loving energies are being directed to you at the same time! What message do you receive from the star guardian? What image do you receive? What word comes to mind? What feeling? Take your time. Relax. See what comes. Feel the love. Receive cleansing and healing! Now turn your energies in the direction of Gaia, the soul of our troubled Planet Earth. Feel her distress at the pollution which blankets the planet. See her anger and frustration that humankind does not love her nor treat her with respect and reverence. Send love to her. Send healing to her. Tell her that you will help her recover and flourish in a new, risen frequency.

Allow your heart and soul to travel toward Gaia's most beautiful and powerful aspects. Mighty mountains. Wild, rolling seas. Deep green forests alive with life. Send her healing energies once again. Feel your white quartz, which is very warm now, pulsing with your positive and wonderful energy.

Take a deep breath. Open your eyes. Lovingly place your white quartz in front of you, blessing it with God's love as you do so. Feel the golden/white light of goodness once more. The meditation is over.

Four Elements Meditation

The following meditation is most effective in working with Gaia.

Designate four objects to symbolize the Four Elements. We recommend that you obtain a feather to represent Air.

A piece of burned wood can represent Fire. A simple, small bowl of water can represent Water. And, a bit of soil from a special area can represent Earth. If you prefer, you can use a lighted candle to represent Fire, but we find it tends to dominate the meditation. Candles are dynamic for meditation in themselves, however, and when using one, you must always remember that you are communicating with the Element Fire, who has a living essence.

Begin your meditation as usual. Open spiritual channels. Wash yourself in good intent and positive outcome. Now place the feather at the top of your circle. It also represents The North. Put the burned wood to the right within the circle. It also represents East. Place a bit of earth at the bottom of your circle. It represents South. Finally, place the bowl of water to the left within the circle. It represents West.

Allow to come what will. Relax, keep spiritual channels open. Concentrate on the feather. Say, "Air cleanses All. Wind, blow away all sadness."

Now concentrate on the burned wood. Say, "Fire fans the flames of life. Burn, Fire."

Now concentrate on the bit of earth. Say, "Earth is mother of All. Bless the Earth!" Now concentrate on the bowl of water. Say, "Water washes the old away and brings life anew."

"Air, Fire, Earth, Water, work for me now, help me bring The Light!"

Run your hand clockwise around the circle four times. Think/feel, "Air," on the first circuit, "Fire," on the second, "Earth," on the third, and "Water," on the fourth circuit. Now, go ahead with a less structured meditation or walk in nature, and see what comes to you!

A Healing Meditation for You

This meditation is for health problems which may keep you from enjoying life as well as from fulfilling your spiritual purpose. We realize it is difficult to help the planet when you are not feeling well yourself.

There is a knock-on (domino) effect with this kind of health concern: For instance, if you have allergies, you may also have chronic headaches. And this can lead to depression. If you are depressed, you might notice a backache, whereas if you were busy and fulfilled, you wouldn't notice it as much.

It doesn't help to say that some health problem may be "psychosomatic," because, in fact, all ailments of the physical vessel are ultimately mind controlled and connected. So it does little good to say, "Oh, it's in your mind."

Certainly allergies have an outside factor, the planet's atmosphere is becoming less breathable by the day. A backache isn't automatically "in the mind," either, as there can be strain or injury from outside. The point is, it does no good to categorize any specific ailment as "in the mind." It is all more complex than that.

But the mind can control pain and even the source of the problem to a huge degree (we speak especially of nonterminal, chronic ailments). The mind can do this through the right healing meditation.

Like finding the way home, the ultimate answer lies within you. Yes, you can go to a healer once, but you cannot bring the healer home with you on a daily basis. You therefore have yourself as your constant and best healer.

Unfortunately, "you" is sometimes the source of the ailment as well. So, The Healer You must overcome the make-you-sick you.

The object for this meditation is that The Healer You will enter your areas of concern within your body, and establish balance where there is now imbalance. We know there is imbalance because they are problem areas.

The focus of this meditation is to achieve balance within, and to plug energy leaks. We urge you to use a green healing stone, such as Irish Connemara Marble or a Moss Green Agate. Deep blue Lapis Lazuli is also a good gemstone helpmate on this meditation. Place the gemstone on the area of concern. For instance, if you have more than your share of headaches, lie down on your back and place the gemstone on your forehead. This can be done during a headache or as a preventative measure. The gemstone centers The Healer You on the sight of the problem. The Healer You enters the body and finds the area from which precious energy is leaking or spilling out. The Healer You discovers the area of imbalance.

With warm, vibrant green (or blue), healing energy, wash this area thoroughly with the strong thought of restoring balance. Keep washing until balance is *felt*. It will be like the perfect, clear, pure, stillness of a pond.

You may do this many times, or once. You may want this to last only a few minutes or for an hour or so if you wish to rest or take a nap. It is good to fall asleep doing this meditation.

The object is not to dominate the negative, but to eliminate its domination by restoring balance and plugging the energy leak. The color of the healing energy depends on what gemstone you are using, but the principle healing force is The Healer You.

Meditation closed.

Mother, I feel you under my feet.
Mother, I feel your heartbeat
Mother, I feel your touch

This is a beautiful invocation to Gaia which you may use in meditation in a number of ways. "Father" may be used also, of course, when you are addressing The Sky Father (God).

CHAPTER TWENTY-ONE: A FINAL WORD FROM TIBUS

This is Tibus. I come to you in love and light.

If I were to choose one cornerstone of my teachings, it would be that a relatively small group of enlightened souls can make a huge difference in future reality simply through the psychic/spiritual power of their united minds.

My entire mission regarding Earth, late Twentieth Century, is built on this firm belief. But I am not alone in this belief!

All of us within The Space/Dimensional Intelligence believe this also. You have hinged your human mission on this truth. Before you became a human being in the present lifetime, you were on the Home Side with us, and you agreed to be a member of this small but brave and determined group of human beings.

This group realizes that the planet is in severe trouble, that Earth Changes are occurring dramatically, and that the silver lining of a higher dimension of existence is possible!

Reality is built on how one's consciousness perceives the dimensional overlay. Mass consciousness consists of an entire race (the human race in this case), perceiving reality in a certain way, thus functioning on a certain frequency. The subatomic molecules of consciousness do not dictate that reality be created in one way or another. Consciousness particles are simply building blocks; a race (a world), can build those blocks any way it chooses.

But after a while, the dominant race on the planet (the human race), believes that the reality which has been constructed is the only reality there is, and that particles of consciousness are molded in unchangeable stone.

Nothing could be further from the truth nor from what The Creator intended. The Creator loves creativity and diversity. In fact, The Creator is creation itself! A race must reach a point of awareness when it realizes it can knock down the old, low frequency which is crumbling (unravelling), anyway, and build a beautiful new reality out of the same sparks of consciousness.

This is in essence what our **Star Network** does even now. And it is, in essence, what we are asking all readers of this book.

If certain catastrophic, negative events are strong possibilities in your upcoming timeline, then enlightened people can change the future so that these events are weakened or do not happen at all. Enlightened people can scatter the molecules of a negative reality using their psychic power. Some crisis can be averted totally while others can only be lessened (no one can bat 100 percent). We can only try our best.

The Half Full Glass

It is difficult to appreciate that which does *not* happen. Remember our analogy to a fender bender car accident? A fatal traffic accident did not happen, yet we are upset with even a fender bender. Perceiving the half-full glass is a cornerstone of psychic power. The half-empty glass is self-defeating.

You can affect molecules of consciousness, which are the fabric of Space/Time, in a positive way. As you (and we), weave a positive alternate reality, healing occurs, for other lifeforms, for the planet, and even for yourself. The positive alternate reality becomes self-perpetuating.

Set it in motion! Belief, hope, and trust in the future, these are the psychic reinforcements and enhancements of the fabric of the positive future reality. Join us in the promise of the risen frequency!

As I travel my universal path. I look forward to working with you, shoulder to shoulder, as we strive to save our beautiful Mother Planet, and to raise the frequency.

May the healing light of God and goodness surround you, always,

Tibus

Hello, this is Diane with a last word.

There is little I can add to what Tibus has just said. It is my fervent belief that Earth will make it through these days of Earth Change. I admit, when one looks at the many threats to our survival, it can be disheartening. But if we become disheartened, it seems to spell our own demise. That is just common sense as well as good metaphysics.

I have worked with our friends of The Space/Dimensional Intelligence for fourteen years now on a conscious basis, and I can only repeat: I am positive we will make it through these Change Times! I have certain knowledge of this, from our higher friends, and from within my own mind and soul.

But, there will be sweeping changes. Survival will be a challenge, both physically and spiritually. However, when we awaken our deep spiritual nature, we are helped toward physical survival, too.

We as a race have forgotten that we can create our own new reality; the society keeps us too busy paying the rent and bringing home groceries to remember this ancient truth. We are caught in our own trap!

Let's free ourselves! We are soon to be *cosmic citizens.* We are a powerful and good race, and only we can save our world. Certainly this is preferable to destroying our world and ourselves in the process.

The great bonus is, while you are saving your world, you are healed and helped as an individual. Your own psychic power is freed so as you can create a better reality for yourself, too. Our fate is tied to the Mother Planet's fate, and her fate is tied to ours. Let's not let that statement be bad news, let's allow it to be the best news in the galaxy!

This is the first in a series of three books. We look forward to further communication.

Special thanks to my co-workers, the star people, who have believed in our message for fourteen years. Their love, friendship, and support have been truly miraculous. They have made this book possible. Special thanks to Gaia herself, who has been my friend forever; with her, I am never alone. She is pure magic! Special thanks to Della, Tim, Vincent, and Briege, whose friendships are golden. Last but not least, thanks to Gianna, Joshua, Sinsee, and The Pooka.

Diane Tessman
P.O. Box 1802
Joshua Tree, California 92252-0857

Feel free to contact me.

FOR MORE INFORMATION...

The Change Times Quarterly available directly from Diane Tessman, is published four times a year with urgent transmissions by Tibus, Alexander, Veritan, Amethysta, Celiera, Micha, Ashtar, and other members of The Space/Dimensional Intelligence. The most current global situations are discussed and crucial information is given. Don't miss out! This is a *must* for enlightened people!

Find out the real news. Discover what you must do to protect yourself, find out what you can do to help. 20 packed pages four times a year! We warned of Ebola, the deadly new disease, over a year before it made news headlines. **CTQ** warned of a series of deadly train crashes in 1996, long before they began to occur. Volcano, earthquake, ozone alerts, violent storm warnings, constitute amazingly accurate information, often given beforehand, which is indispensable to you personally.

Censored from the regular news media, CTQ contains insights on the big news events and updates on what missions our Space/Dimensional friends are currently involved. Prophecy, prediction, and the real story makes this publication one you must subscribe to! There is a lot of good news, too, a lot of hope. "Each issue is more incredible and helpful than the one before. I can't wait until the next one comes out!" Sharon Kennedy, Albany, N.Y.

Subscription price for **CTQ** is $45.00 per year (4 issues)
If you buy each issue as a single, each issue is $12.00
Diane sends your copy personally, always sent first class.

The Star Network Heartline is personally written, channeled, and published monthly by Diane Tessman. **The Heartline** is a precious friend to light workers all over the globe, working as a personal helpmate and inspiration. Dates for our important Cleansing/Healing Days are always listed in **The Heartline** urgent channelings are received from Tibus and other Space/Dimensional friends. There are timely features to give you new strength and good fortune; you will receive confirmation month after month that you are not alone down here! $25.00 per year, 12 issues.

We offer **Starlight Mystic Awareness Lessons**. You may order a sample for $2.00, just let Diane know.

We also offer a number of invaluable **Cosmic Manuscripts** written by Diane and Tibus on vital subjects. Send for our $2.00 Catalog!

Wonderful Audio and Video Tapes by Diane Tessman which you will cherish, also available. Send for our $2.00 Catalog!

Allow Diane to choose and energize just the right gemstone or crystal for you, or to give you a personal, private channeling, with Tibus' help. Write for details! Feel free to write us at:

Diane Tessman
P.O. Box 1802
Joshua Tree, California 92252-0857

TUELLA'S FINAL WORK UPON THE EARTH PLANE IS NOW AVAILABLE FROM INNER LIGHT PUBLICATIONS

A New Book of Revelations

● OUR FATHER UNVEILS THE GRAND DECEPTION FOR THE "LAST DAYS"

WARNING: THIS WORK CORRECTS MANY OF THE MISCONCEPTIONS AND INACCURATE TRANSLATIONS MADE IN THE OLD AND NEW TESTAMENTS AND LAYS A FOUNDATION FOR A *NEW* "BOOK OF REVELATIONS" AS TRANSCRIBED FROM THE HIGHEST SPIRITUAL POWERS IN THE UNIVERSE.

Originating from the *Celestial Throne,* the messages contained in this book represent the joint energies of the Father's Messengers delivered at a very chaotic time in our planet's history and offers an important NEW BEGINNING for all of humankind.

SOME OF THE SHOCKING REVELATIONS INCLUDE:

- The TRUE meaning of 666.
- The special significance of the 13th Vortex.
- How the primary channel for this work was able to thwart the forces of darkness and thus facilitate the departure of the "fallen ones" from the West Coast.
- How God's rebellious son Jehovah inserted distortions into the original biblical scriptures to create disharmony and strife among God's children.
- How the "fallen ones" plan to enslave humanity and in which nation "the beast" will rise to power.
- How a legion of Angels will protect you personally during a global war that will take place in the Middle East in the not-so-distant future.

NOW IS THE TIME TO GET READY FOR THE GREAT CHANGES TO HAPPEN IN OUR LIFETIME.

160 pages $15.00

This book represents the apex of Tuella's mission on Earth. According to God (channeled by Tuella), Jehovah tampered with the encodements of Divine Revelation and "as a result the entire Creation has become a battleground for men's minds, a battle of the truth against the false, the Light against the dark, the whole against the broken truth." Tuella was told: "We must change the codes back to their divine state and this is what is represented by your writing." It is now vital that this information be set straight for "the time now approaches so closely to those days described therein, we must now act quickly to release this information for the benefit of My Children, upon whom this clever deceiver shall focus his attention.

THESE TITLES ALSO AVAILABLE BY TUELLA—PRIMARY REPRESENTATIVE OF THE ASHTAR COMMAND

PROJECT WORLD EVACUATION

UFOs are here to assist in the "Great Exodus" of Human Souls off this planet predicted to occur by the year 2000! Where will the rescued be taken? Who will qualify?

160 pgs.—$15.00

ON EARTH ASSIGNMENT

The Cosmic Awakening of Light Workers—Walk-Ins and All Star-Born Representatives has begun! Find out what your special mission is to be as the planet is swept into a higher level of consciousness.

176 pgs.—$15.00

THE DYNAMICS OF COSMIC TELEPATHY

A Workbook and study guide to expanding your inner clairvoyant powers. Now it's possible for humankind to cross barriers of space and time.

160 pgs.—$15.00

ASHTAR—REVEALING THE SECRET PROGRAM OF THE FORCES OF LIGHT AND THEIR SPIRITUAL PROGRAM ON EARTH

The name Ashtar has become widely known in UFO channeling circles for several decades. It is aid that his messages are being beamed from a colossal Starship—or Space Station—beyond our atmosphere.

168 pgs.—$18.00

COSMIC PROPHECIES FOR YEAR 2000

World chaos. World changes. Arrival of the guardians of the world. Earth—a planet in peril. Trial by fire.

168 pgs.—$18.00

To Order Via Credit Card, Call Our 24-Hour Order Hotline at (908) 602-3407

Mail to: INNER LIGHT PUBLICATIONS, Box 753, New Brunswick, NJ 08903